# The Movement of Life

2521-MARC

# The Movement of Life

## (ESSAYS FROM THE SPIRIT FOR THE SPIRIT)

*ভৈ*

## TESS MARCIN

To order additional copies of this book, contact:
Xlibris Corporation
1-888-7-XLIBRIS
www.Xlibris.com
Orders@Xlibris.com

# Contents

## BY THE SAME AUTHOR

Move That Horizon
From Another Angle
Hey! Remember Me? I'm Back . . .
Make Your Day
You Don't Need A Bodhi Tree
Living the Cycle Within the Circle
The Movement Of Life

# Dedication

## TO MY FAMILY

My sons

Tom, Jerry, David

My daughters-in-law

Dixie, Stace

My granddaughter

Danni

With love

2521-MARC

# PREFACE

## *THE "WORD" IS LIFE*

LIFE is a circle
LIFE is a cycle
LIFE is a given and Life is given
LIFE is a gift
LIFE is a passage and LIFE is passed on
LIFE is a seed that grows, that perpetuates itself
LIFE is for the moment and LIFE is eternal
LIFE is a lesson and LIFE is an experience
LIFE is what you make of it and LIFE is what it makes
of you
LIFE is a stream and LIFE is a well
LIFE is a movement and LIFE motivates
LIFE is a dance, it is a "DANSE ESPIRITU" and LIFE
is a "DANSE MACABRE"
LIFE, without it we would not be
LIFE is the "WORD"
THE "WORD" is "LIFE"
THE MOVEMENT OF LIFE

# INTRODUCTION

We all live the life we were given, and it is a life in motion. Life has never been known to stand still, it moves in and it moves out, life controls the flow. But within that flow we are the ones who decide what craft to row down the river, or to motor down the river, or even to just float down the river without any craft. The craft, the method, are the choices we make as we live life within its parameters.

We search for knowledge, we look for wisdom, we seek insight, enlightenment, and we do all this as individuals. We pick our method, we establish our belief, we practice our faith, and we do all this within the confines of life's movement.

We may be able to see, to feel, to realize, what our choices have wrought, the good and the bad. Then again in the eternality of life such insight, such enlightenment, such realization, may not come to us during this cycle.

To experience the lesson's of life is the project we were given, and the human has his ups and downs within the experiences. One thing we cannot say for certain is that the human has learned anything.

Given the estimated age of the human which is some 4.6 billion years if one uses the yardstick of the Genesis; and also if one enters into the equation the estimates of the age of this planet by our scientists; time has not made us into perfect humans. Taking the status of our world into consideration and the antics of the human up to this point, it would seem man is not a good caretaker of himself or his abode. He finds it hard to learn what life is trying to teach.

What will it take for man to reverse his direction? It will need each individual to just quit floating down the river of life and to pay more attention to the craft he is using.

Insight begins when each person realizes that the responsibility begins and ends with the self.

To man it is time, to life it is simply a movement.

# ONE

## *LOOKING WITHIN*

It is not out there, it is here. Life is lived in this moment of time, and time is measured from one breath unto the next. Within the now of that breath is the cycle of the life as known to man.

Every living soul lives only in that space known as . . . now.

We may think we know the direction, but we are all lost souls. To find ourselves, to find our way, to move forward, is the destiny of each individual.

And how do we find the direction? We ask. And whom do we ask? The Supreme Being. He is the keeper of all directions. He is the keeper of all doors. He is the keeper of all keys.

And what is the direction we are given? To look within, to go within.

The true journey must always begin within the self.

And when one seeks the inner, what does one find? One finds there aren't any barriers, any walls, any parameters, any limits. One finds insight, one finds enlightenment, one finds wisdom, one finds infinity, one finds eternality, one finds self, and one finds the way.

The awakening begins, here is where it starts.

521-MARC

# TWO

## *EVOLVING MAN*

When we speak of the movement of life, many times we fail to take into consideration what this really means.

Life, movement, energy, things happen within that movement that are beyond our control. Who among us can control his dreams, his thoughts, his feelings, his "life," his so-called death? Certainly man tries, but like trying to stop the wind from blowing, it's an effort in futility.

So as we pursue what we refer to as the reality of this life, we must accept the "unreality" that comes from within. As we live both, we create our history for today.

We live this life as humans, we use the robe of matter to define ourselves. Science has searched long and hard to explain the intangibles that contribute to the life of the human and his body. They believe they have the answer as to how the body works, but the explanation for the intangibles might as well be written on the wind.

Science in trying to explain humanity seems to skip over the individual that is a part of it. They fail to see the uniqueness of him, and also find it impossible to trace and define this uniqueness.

Science has taken apart the human body, almost cell by cell, it believes it knows its construct intimately. It doesn't. It has yet to discover the "chain" that makes each individual so unique. Sure, science makes reference to genes, to hereditary, but to isolate the chain, to isolate the movement of life, as it makes its way through its hereditary chain, is still a mystery.

Man looks at himself in the mirror and sees the person he calls "I," but is what he sees just "I?" What is it made of? Even our modern day computers would find it difficult to come up with a definitive answer, a conclusive, complete one.

The movement of life is not only an individual one, it is a genealogical one. Genealogy has come a long way, it has many devotees. The search for one's ancestors is as interesting as any mystery novel. The novel comes to an end, the ancestral search goes on.

Each baby as it comes into this world is already an "I." As it goes through life this is the word of reference to the self. This is an identifying word, along with whatever name it has been given. But beyond the molecular structure, beyond the cells, the housing, there is more than just an, "I." There is a biological chain that stretches back in time, as well as before time.

The little baby is a complex individual. It has not only the genes of its parents, it has the genes of its grandparents, on both sides. It has genes from every ancestor within that direct chain. So as it goes through life referring to itself as "I," it also is making reference to "we," "to us," because it is more than a singular "I." It is many rolled into this one entity and it will live its life with "all."

As the child grows up, as it lives that life, when it has children, the "chain" will continue. If there aren't any children, the chain may seem broken, is it? Is its uniqueness gone? What happens when such a soul, such a spirit, ceases to exist in "life?" Does its eternal "life" also cease, does it no longer go around within the circle or climb the spiral? Or does its soul, its spirit merely move back across the threshold and pick up a new cycle? A new "chain?"

Science acknowledges the human, how could it not, and the "life" of the human as it exists today. Science has a problem recognizing this life as also existing before being enrobed in matter. It is perfectly willing to attribute 4.6 billion years to the age of this sphere called Earth, but it is hesitant to include the human. It bases its conjectures on how the Earth was formed, the initial atmosphere, vegetation, and places the animals in residence before the human. This lack of foresight or hindsight or any sight, does not enhance its credibility. If the Earth is billions of years old and it sustained life in the form of vegetation, in animal life, it also must have sustained life in human form.

Science places the appearance of man in the period called the "Stone Age." A very short-sighted placement.

There is life and there is "Life" and "Life" in matter has been around before.

What is puzzling is the definition of human life as seen by the scientific world. Many would have us believe that the movement called life either first crawled out of the sea or evolved from apes. How can they rationalize this way of think? And why do so many buy it?

To say man evolved from apes, or evolved from something from the ocean, is not sustainable thinking.

Taking those 4.6 billion years into consideration, or even ignoring them, has such a phenomena occurred within the memory of man? Hardly, no matter how closely one looks, apes remain apes, and the sea creature still retains its form and lives in the sea. It has never grown a human body no matter how long its been under the microscope of the scientific world. Evolution may be an evolving, but it is an evolvement of like into like. One cannot take the fact that there is a spine, organs, or whatever features that seem to resemble man's, as a reason to say man evolved from something. A similarity of base is present in all life, it is part of the format.

Man, when he came into being, was given an intelligence, far beyond anything an ape has or a fish, but sometimes he uses this intelligence to come up with conjectures with theories, that make the gift of intelligence seem wasted on the human.

Stone Age man, however he was clothed, whatever he looked like, was still a man, not an ape. He was creative, he could express himself, crudely perhaps, but expressing none the less. He had a personality, he had values, he was biologically capable of producing another "human."

It seems the world of science, having strayed down a certain path, is reluctant to return because its future credibility might be questioned. So it has decided to hew to the path of no return rather than take a new more enlightened one. News flash! Its creditability is already in doubt.

Man has lived all over this planet, not any of it is untouched virgin territory. Man has left his mark, nature has left hers. What we call our environment has undergone tremendous change. In some areas more slowly, in others catyclismically, but as man continues his evolvement, so does the planet he occupies. Change, or whatever one wishes to call it, is taking place according to plan. Man can do nothing to stop it.

Modern man's intellect has created a space program. It has landed him on the moon, it has allowed him to put an invention on Mars, it has given him the ability to send probes far beyond what can be seen in our skies.

The mechanism on Mars is capable of taking pictures and sending them back to Earth to be evaluated. Our problem, it cannot move beyond a certain radius. It cannot touch, feel, smell. It is tiny, so everything around it looks huge. What it has sent back is interesting, but limited in scope. If someone from another planet had landed a similar device in our Bad Lands, our desert, or any such areas anywhere on the globe, it would have sent back to its inventors a skewed outlook of our planet. Conversely, if it had landed in New York City, the pictures would tell a different story. What lies on the backside of Mars? What lies underneath its surface? Is there life, but not life as we view it through our eyes?

Tiny "Sojourner" did make the discovery that Mars was once inhabited, that it had life but if its inhabitants were human, like us, or human in some other form, has not come to light. Mars is said to be much older than the Earth. Something happened on it or to it to make it barren, will our planet resemble it a few billion years from now? Will someone, at that time, say this planet had never been occupied?

Yes, we live the movement of life as "humans" today, but before we became humans we existed totally in spirit. Anyone who chooses not to believe this truth probably also does not believe in life eternal. To them if it can't be touched, can't be felt, it isn't viable, it hasn't any validity. A discrediting type of think, since it negates the human himself. Spirit lives, even if it is beyond visibility The movement of life does not just take place in the now, it encompasses the past and the future. It encompasses the cycles of the human life, and the off ramps of life beyond the human.

Yes, man has lived on this planet for millions and billions of years. He has changed its face, he has altered the environment. Each new generation that comes along leaves its mark in some fashion. Each generation does its thing and moves on, the footprints they leave behind existing for but a very short time.

Just as we cannot see what took place when the humans in our past lived on this planet, so we cannot see what changes will take place in the future. The ashes of the past, the dust of the future, both present in the human that lives today.

Today man is urged to conserve, to take care of his environment, nature looks at his puny efforts and in one fell swoop changes what surrounds man. Who is more destructive, man or nature?

This planet will not survive because of man, nor will it disappear because of him.

The movement of life takes place in nature, in the human. Changes take place with or without their help.

Yes, man was given dominion over all he surveys and his very existence demands change if he is to survive. He must build that shelter, he must till that soil, he must put food on the table, he must provide for his safety, his security. He must provide for self. As he goes about living this life, he must use what the planet provides in a careful manner.

Yes, man was given dominion, but dominion should not be the precursor to wholesale destruction. Those who lived before made changes, but it is possible that they also practiced a necessary restraint. If they had not would planet Earth still be a viable, livable sphere? After 4.6 billion years, the movement of life does create change. Of a kind.

Modern man has done more damage in his short span than man who lived in the many millennia's of the past.

Never, as far as we know, has man appeared in such numbers. Man was told to multiply, has he overdone it? Man was given the ability to be creative, has he gone too far?

Our society refers to itself as being civilized, and as a society we feel in order to live this life we need more . . . of everything. In the pursuit of everything will we have outsmarted ourselves? Man was given dominion, he was granted intelligence, as he makes his way down the stream of life, will he finally see the light?

With man or without man, the movement of life will continue. Life is perpetual motion, and it doesn't just surround us, life doesn't have any parameters. Time does not contain it, time does not define it. Life just is, it is movement without end.

# THREE

## *BEEN THERE . . . DONE THAT*

Life is movement. When one hears someone say, in today's vernacular, "Been there . . . Done that," does thought stop at the phrase or does it move beyond it?

Almost all who utter it, almost all who hear it, are thinking of life today, and what they have experienced, and are experiencing while living it. And yet it really goes beyond the present, it encompasses the past, as well as including the future.

As we live our eternal life, as we move up the spiral, in and out of the circle, we truly have been there, and have done it all. We are reliving what we call the past and we are living the future. Our "memories" come to the fore in all events of the past, the present, the future. The path of destiny continues to reveal itself.

As an analogy we could use the tree. It is past, it is present, it is the future, and it stands in the moment of its own eternality. The seed, the tree, the growth period, the dormant time, and again the seed, the tree, the growth, on and on and on . . .

Of course, the tree does not have a "human" memory, but it does have its own built in "memory." It remembers how to live its "life." We can cut down the tree, we can burn it, it can dry up, many things can happen to it, but there is always a seed left behind for it to carry on.

To presume to explain how God operates, what His intent is, what He is, is the human ego working at top pitch. It is wishful thinking that makes the human venture down this path. The human thinks he has the answer, but he doesn't even know the question. His talent, his gift, his ability, did not come only as part of the package called human, it is part of his spirit and yet with all this he was not given the insight that would allow him to explain his Creator.

So the human, not knowing the question, begins a search for his roots, his human heritage. As he searches he soon discovers that his true roots are not of this world. Before arriving as a human, he was spirit. His memory cannot bridge this gap so when he says, "Been there . . . Done that," he can only refer to his cyclical life as a human. His cyclical life as spirit in another dimension eludes his memory.

His roots . . . in time, and out of time.

His memory . . . selective.

# FOUR

## *KNOW THYSELF*

One of the most quoted phrases is, "Know thyself." Easier said than done, inasmuch as it refers to an individual setting out to accomplish this task. Many opt instead to find someone to do the job for them. In other words they seek an "expert." Now if anyone stops to analyze what is happening here, they'll soon be aware of the contradiction, the fallacy of such a venture.

To "Know thyself" is a singular action. It is a personal journey, an inward journey, in search of what makes one tick, and the reason that ticking occurs. To accompany the phrase "Know thyself," we have, "Seek and ye shall find."

Neither phrase instructs one to seek advice from those who deem themselves experts, purveyors of nonaction. The seeker, in their presence, finds himself stumbling around searching mind to verbally toss words into the silence offered by such purveyors.

They may be able to listen, but they cannot help, and they can do harm. One can do more for oneself by sitting in front of a mirror and addressing the image one sees.

One may spout whatever comes to mind while in the presence of some "expert," one can spout the same words while addressing one's own image. What one soon discovers is that while one can lie to the "expert," make up fanciful tales, salve one's ego, one cannot look into one's own eyes in the mirror and lie to one's ownself. Why? Because the self is who one is and the self knows what is going on.

When one looks at one's self in the mirror, one faces reality. This is who one is, this is who one has created, and if one wishes to change, this is where one begins. While looking into the eyes in the mirror one sees the reflection of the inner world of self.

The self looks out at one and silently informs one, "You took all the actions, you made all the choices, you allowed your ego prominence of first place. You may feel that others influenced you, but you allowed it. Observe your creation. Know the self you are so you can change the self you are. No one else can do it for you."

Yes, "Know thyself" is a search within, and no one else can know what is there.

No one can teach what one must learn for self.

One is one's own "expert."

# FIVE

## *THE DIVERSITY OF MOVEMENT*

The movement of life is represented in diverse ways. As life itself is energy that is ever on the move, so are the many facets that come under its heading.

Communication, dialogue, philosophical discussion, etc., are part of the movement. We could even say, the first sound made by the first human was movement being brought forth. Man became so intrigued by the sound of his voice that to this day he continues to keep his tongue in motion. Man seeks to teach himself, not only as an individual, but as part of humanity as a whole. Has he come to a definitive conclusion? Not at all, he keeps expanding his arena of movement, the ripples keep spreading and how far they will spread is an unknown.

So the verbal movement continues. The opinions, the perspectives, the beliefs, go on and on. Man keeps looking for himself, he keeps looking for what he calls a being, he acknowledges the spirit, but man has not managed to locate, to pin point, to find, to touch, what he seeks.

The verbal movement, the action of the tongue as it seeks to communicate is visible, the action has been defined but what about the words being uttered? Yes, they are formed, yes they are heard, yes, they are part of the movement of life, but they are just as ephemeral as spirit. No one has ever touched a word, felt the word. Like the air it is wafted on, it disappears, and no one knows where. Communication took place, but where did it go?

The force of life, the energy of life, life and its movement, known and yet unknown. Can't be seen, can't be touched, and yet, there it is. Where? Everywhere!

The movement of life . . .

The diversity of its movement . . .

Faith in action.

# SIX

## *CHANGE IS MOVEMENT*

The movement of life is change in action. It affects and it effects.

Man must accept change, man must accept its challenges and its frustrations. When change occurs simply as part of normal life man cannot do much about it. But change also takes place by the action of choice, of decision. This is the type of change under the control of man.

As man lives with the change that is beyond his control and as he lives with the change that is within his control, he often feels as if he were going in two different directions.

Change begins the day man is born. Man changes, in some way, every second of his life until his final second. Such change is controlled by destiny. The flow, the movement of life, carries man along with it until he meets his final movement.

Man fears this type of change. He spends his days trying to hold the flow back. He ignores the fact that trying to hold the movement back is futile. Man gets so frustrated at being unable to slow the flow, or to stop it, that he forgets to live in the flow. He misses the joy it offers, he misses the experience of it. He has life, but is not living it.

The man, who by choice, sets out to live it, gains by the experience. The movement of life doesn't just sweep him along, he uses the idiosyncrasies of the river to gain by them. He adds to his life, but does not dwell on what he cannot control. He chooses his options.

The man, who by choice sets out to live his life, may make errors in judgment, may make mistakes, but he keeps moving. He may not view such as gaining experience, or learning lessons, but whether he realizes it or not, he is going about his life as he was meant to do.

He is learning about the self, while adding to the spiritual self. The spirit, that is living through the human, is learning what such a life is all about.

How can the human, his spirit, tell what is to be learned? Simply by watching the self as it goes through each day, living this life. It must exercise patience. Many today have a hard time with this.

They are impatient when they have to wait. They are impatient when they can't get what they want.

They are impatient every day, all day.

Do they gain by this? Hardly!

Impatience causes frustration and it feeds on itself.

Impatience is a choice.

Impatience hastens the flow of the river.

Man was born with the ability for compassion, it is his choice to use it or not. Today compassion has different connotations. It has acquired the "me" angle. It has become self-oriented. Compassion is a two-way street, if one doesn't practice it, one doesn't receive it. "Do unto others as you would have them do unto you . . ." A tenet within the movement of life.

Self-discipline, responsibility, for the self, by the self, if man continues to disregard such, surely the movement of life, the cycle of life, will bring him back for another try.

The movement of life, its changes occur on all levels, they occur to all mankind. It is up to the human, when faced with a choice, to make it a wise one. It may be the one lesson he was sent here to learn.

Life is change, change is life. It will brighten or it will darken man's outlook. If man uses it to light the life of fellowman, than the movement of life will have defined itself.

# SEVEN

## *THE GIFT WITH STRINGS*

Life demands. Life demands much from us as individuals. It is a gift with strings.

Life did come with our spirit and along with the energy of life, we received will. Will can be looked at as a birthright, but it really should be looked at as a gift that came with birth. As a gift it cannot be a right.

We also received the gift of choice. Choice is a responsibility. Ability and talent were given us to enable us to grow our selves. Through the human, spirit experiences.

Life, will, choice, responsibility, ability, talent. When one receives so many gifts, one soon ceases to look at them with awe, with gratefulness. Like a child at its own birthday party or during the holidays, there is so much, that the eyes glaze over and all is taken for granted, certainly it is not appreciated.

So life has embedded, within its "structure," demands. These demands are like a wake-up call, they are meant to wake one up, arouse one, make one aware. The dues, for being allowed to join the club of life, will come due periodically, during the tenure of life. As one lives life, as one pays attention to those dangling strings and as one takes advantage of the gifts, one must use them judiciously.

Using the will is power in action. To use it to grow the inner self is the highest goal. When it is used against one's own ilk it can be degrading, demoralizing, destructive.

Using choice is also an action. Choice helps one's spirit progress, it enables it to experience the "experiment" of life. It gives reality to the reason for being. But choice has two sides. Choose the negative and one draws to the dark side of the ego much that is detrimental. Choose the light, the positive side, and benefits accrue.

Using ability, using talent, and using them in a positive manner, not only enhances the life of one's own spirit, it can enhance the life of humankind.

Using responsibility wisely, using it in all aspects of living, makes the demands of life easier to take. Responsibility cannot be shoved aside, because life itself is a responsibility.

Life was given as gift.

Life demands one be responsible for this gift.

Life is not a right.

Life has its own agenda

# EIGHT

## *A GYRATING ACTION*

The world today seems as if it is spinning out of control, but if one views this in perspective one discovers there really isn't any validity in such thinking.

The world, the globe, earth, is 4.6 billion years old, or it could be triple that amount, no one knows. The count-down isn't over either. The world has been around for a mighty long time and it has survived all that nature has imposed on it, it is a tough old sphere.

The human, you, me, we, us, have been around, on this planet, for a like amount of time. The scientists have given an age to this planet, the Genesis has given an age to man. Both created within the "time span" of one week. We say "one week" or "six days" or whatever, but that is a human time frame. It could have all happened within the time span of a snap of God's "fingers."

Now all this should give anyone pause. Our spirit is not of the moment, for the moment, and when it is endowed with "life," it is we, as humans, who live that life.

God created, He is still creating, He will always be creating.

God created the human, He gave him life, He set man on the path of life and He sat back to see what the human would create, would do with this life. Well what the human has done should not come as any surprise. The evidence surrounds us.

We, as humans, have been living life.

Whatever has motivated us has been arrived at by individual choice. The choice of spirit, the choice of self, the choice of ego, someone, or something, was doing the choosing. But it was an inner occurring choice and we cannot blame others for the outcome as choice became reality.

When we, as humans, say the world is spinning out of control, we are evading the true fact, that it is the human race, doing the gyrating.

We are living the life we created for ourselves.

We live the life we continue to create for ourselves.

# NINE

## *ACCEPTING WHO WE ARE*

Once we all accept that living this life in a responsible manner is our duty, we can move on and truly live it.

We create the record here on earth, we take with us the experience gained when we move on. We evaluate it while in the world of spirit and we decide if we learned anything by it. The learning experience, the lesson, is not always a negative, nor is it a positive, it is a combination. One must experience both if one wishes to grow in spirit, grow the spirit, so it can move on.

Psychotherapy has become a panacea for many who seek to avoid responsibility for their actions in the now. Has anyone ever done a really in-depth study of its proported benefits? Could these benefits be self-delusional? Anyone can say they see a truth, even when they do not, it's known as a personal perspective.

Searching a past to explain an action of today can harm. Taking the spirit one is today, and saying it was Mother, Father, Son, Daughter, Husband, Wife, in a previous life? The connotations for the life of today do not bear thinking about. Can this be why our newspapers, our T.V's, are filled with deeds of man gone mad?

Past-life therapy establishing notions without validity, doing much damage in pursuing these notions. Those who seek to absolve themselves of what they see as an emotional problem today, may simply be giving a reality to an illusionary desire. The little girl who says when she grows up she'll marry Daddy. Well, she is grown up now, is the wish, the desire still there? Is it given a reality by assuring her that in a past life it was so? This is a screwed up emotional person allowing themselves to become even more so. Will their entire life now be filled with a moral guilt and will they go from therapist to therapist to assuage that guilt?

Nobody can travel the spirit world of God and state as a fact that the spirits co-mingle, inter-mingle, and assume each others persona. Spirits do not have a gender. Mind does not have a gender. It is the human form that has gender.

Is what is supposedly happening simply too much T.V?

God may grant life to spirit, He may allow that spirit to choose a gender for its human form in this life, so the experience can be a varied one. He may allow racial choice, ethnic choice, but will He allow spirit the choice of what we call incest? Wouldn't this prevent a path of spiritual growth? If such intermingling takes place than man cannot any longer refer to a spirit of self, because self has become a nonentity, it has become a spiritual amoebae, no longer on a separate growth path.

Was Adam the Father of Eve?

Was Eve the Mother of Adam?

We must accept the responsibility of how we live this life, but aren't we stepping over the line by taking this life, which is an ongoing life and looking at a partner, a family, member and saying that is who I was?

Yes, let us accept the responsibility of this life and move on it, that is the destiny of our spirit, to move on. So let's live this life without an overlay of illusionary, delusionary desire.

What does such thinking do to the Ten Commandments?

Spirits are not human, they do not have the attributes of humans.

# TEN

## *GOING WITH THE FLOW*

Moving on is what life is. Has anyone ever tried to hold life back? Has it responded? Did it stand still? Did it go backward? No, life simply kept moving forward.

How many of us believe we know life, know what it means, what it is all about? For those who would like to say they do . . . well, there is that familiar bridge in Brooklyn . . .

The dictionary would like to define it, but who wrote the dictionary, who selected the characters to form the word life? Yes, it was a mortal being, a human, and he defined it as:

Existence; vitality; "the span between birth and death;" mode of living; plus a myriad of other definitions having nothing to do with the life force. And to say it is the span between birth and death, is to ignore the "LIFE" that is eternal.

The human, in attempting a definitive answer, demonstrated he misunderstood the question.

The search for life, the search for its meaning, is wrapped up in its flow.

And who is it that feels he knows the meaning of it, the one out in the world "living" it, or the one in a secluded atmosphere hiding from it?

We all live a life. Life is the energy that flows through us. It makes the heart beat, the blood flow, the lungs expand

and contract. It is the energy the human body needs to function. However there is life and there is "LIFE." And life is the day to day flow, the day to day participation in all that comes its way.

Life has edges, "LIFE" does not. An we as humans are destined to pursue the edgy one. This is the one that creates the experiences, which turn into the lessons that the spirit takes with it in to the abode of the "LIFE" eternal. So life and "LIFE" is movement, only the dimensional flow changes.

We fight for life, that is a basic instinct. The baby that emerges from the Mother's womb has "LIFE," but it must fight for life by gasping for that first breath, and the next, and the next. First lesson . . . The fight for life has begun. The seeking for spiritual fulfillment yet to come.

From birth on, living the life of the human, one goes through many stages. The stages society forces on us to learn, the stages we encounter as we seek self-discovery, self-knowledge. The stages of acceptance, of rejection. We enter the stages, we go through them until we reach that one stage when we realize something seems to be missing. It is within this stage we begin to use reason to define life. Life, as we lived it, may have been dreadful, it may have been exhilarating, but it wasn't completely fulfilling. The process of reasoning has moved us forward, we have reached a point and it is from this point on we begin the search for spiritual fulfillment.

The process of reasoning pointing up what was missing.

Spiritual fulfillment . . .

Yes, there is more to life than mere human existence. There is "LIFE" as defined by our spirit.

Life carries us up to the threshold, "LIFE" carries us over the threshold, spirit keeps moving upward.

# ELEVEN

## *LIVING LIFE*

Moving through life means not being afraid of what it has to offer. So many reject what they hear, or see along the way, simply because they do not know anything about it. They limit their knowledge, they limit their outlook, they box in their life.

We move through life and sometimes life is merely lived within the parameters we have erected. There are many who do not choose to learn how to read and so miss the delights that doing so can bring them. Reading can help one escape those parameters, it can help one see beyond the immediate. When one reads one acquires knowledge, one fills the mind, one allows thought to travel the universe.

One must have an open mind, because when one has an open mind one has opened the doors to the wisdom of one's universe. Beyond the outer, one finds fulfillment in the inner, which allows one to open more doors to the outer. One keeps moving, one keeps knocking, and doors keep opening. Our spiritual forces are always willing to take us in hand and show us a universe without end, the outer as well as the inner. They stir our conscience, which in turn stirs up our consciousness.

Too many fail to explore this hidden dimension of themselves.

We must not be afraid to open the doors to the inner self.

When one is aware of the movement of life and when one is aware of moving through life, one feels as one with the flow of life.

The flow in the evolvement of man, on this planet, is a mere drop in the bucket of the eternal. A planet as seen to be something like 4.6 billion years old (man time), home to man who really cannot be given an age. Man is not aware of the flow, man is only aware of his particular cycle within that time span and this is all he can relate to. Each cycle has been a step up the spiral of spiritual fulfillment as it applies to all humans, as it applies to self. Man has not reached the first curve of the spiral. The time table of man deceives man because it limits man's thinking.

So it is with the spiritual thought of man. Man puts blinders on, he is unwilling to let fellowman see him indulging in such thought. If man would set aside these blinders he would discover the freedom of his conscience. A conscience that roams the eternal, because it is eternal. He will have freed his being.

Man has a tendency to limit the gift of life itself.

Man in limiting what he can be has done himself a disservice.

Man through the ages has attached this leash to himself and he keeps straining at it not realizing it is clipped to his own thought.

Man, today, has chosen something else to attach to the spirit of today. He has attached illnesses of choice. Whether it is because the man of today has more leisure or because his choices are flawed, he has allowed the current fad of any specific illness to attach itself to him. He moves through life using this selection process to reach for anything new that appears on the horizon. He then lives his life pursuing a cure for his ailment of choice. He has picked a bag, filled it with the ailment, flung it over his shoulder and he staggers along wondering what is wrong.

We have, today, the search for the sickness of the spirit, the sickness of the soul. The spirit, the soul, created by the Creator, are not sick. Man created delusions to absolve himself of his true ailment, the ego of man.

Modern science has not done modern man any favors. Ancient man, not being aware of a fraction of such "ailments," never displayed any need to bag an illusion and tote it around. He was too busy trying to keep his life while moving through it. He had his spiritual faith, modern man has abandoned it. He has lost himself looking for an "unreal" world and has not realized the reality of the world of the spiritual self, which even in its reality he views as unreal.

So many today, in trying to escape what this life has to offer, have injected fear into their lives. Fear of this, fear of that. Fear will never move them forward, fear will never blaze a trail, fear will keep them locked up within the parameters they have set for themselves.

They believe they are living life, but life is passing them by as they continue to merely exist.

Living life, as it was meant to be lived . . .

Takes courage.

# TWELVE

## *OBSERVING THE PHOENIX*

The phoenix that rises from the ashes of life, is "LIFE." If nothing else could prove to man that life is eternal, it is this sketch, this picture. "LIFE" doe not end when life ends. The movement does not stop, the flow is not blocked.

Life is in itself a series of essays. Each essay building on the one before it until all culminates in a final burst of effort. And then, no sooner does one burst through, one finds a new cycle beginning.

The human race is filled with discontent. The source? Well, if we take a step back in "time" some billions of years, we may find the reason. It was sometime back then when "spirit" lost Paradise and all it had to offer. Spirit has been searching for it ever since. It is not an impulse that propels "man" in his search, it is a memory.

Paradise was a world of spirit, spirit was fulfilled there. But, when spirit became clothed in matter, it took on a new life. Lessons, experiences, wherever man went spirit had to follow. Man is filled with discontent because spirit wants to go back to Paradise.

Man is attached to earth, to his planet. He has evolved within its confines. Spirit feels hampered by these confines, it seeks to rise above them.

Man, in many respects resembles the phoenix. Within him is life and within him is "LIFE." He rises from his own ashes as spirit eternal. Man would do well to look beyond the planet earth. He would do well to seek the life that is out there. He would do well to follow the movement of the phoenix. There is life beyond planet earth. Nowhere is it written that life must be ensconced in a human form alone. We are said to be created in His image, but who is to say this image is static?

Earth time limits our view, the human limits his perception, alters his perspective. He sees only what he wishes to see

We ride the current, we emerge from the ashes and when we arrive, where are we? We are on the next level, the next plane. We are living the cycles within the circle. The phoenix forever on the rise.

We need only look at our own acclaimed civilization, its society, its cultures, to give credence to the phoenix bird. How many times has civilization risen from its own ashes? Are we moving towards the end of this civilization? And lest anyone gets hung-up on the word civilization and its definition, civilized is in the eye of its beholder. We call ourselves civilized and yet someone from before time might call us barbarians.

Ancient man, modern man, civilized man, turning into ash.

When the next phoenix rises, what will it look like?

# THIRTEEN

## *LIFE TEACHES*

Life teaches, but only what one is willing to learn . . .
Life teaches, and one does not always have a choice in the lesson . . .

Life teaches, it points up the fact that no one knows life . . .
Life teaches . . .

Life does not offer panaceas, man creates these for himself. Man believes they are needed to overcome whatever goes bump in the night. It's like giving candy to a child to help it get over whatever disturbed it or kissing the place where the hurt is to make it go away.

No one can do anything about one's self-image, it was created by one's self.

No one can alter one's perception of life, it is up to one to choose how one views it. One can choose to look through a prism or one can choose to look through a cracked mirror, the reflection from either will differ.

No one can experience life for one, it is not theirs to experience.

Life teaches that our connection with God is solid. It is not an illusion. It is not a delusion.

Life also teaches, that as humans, we tend to deny this connection.

Life teaches that the gift of choice is one that mankind has the most difficulty with.

Life will go on teaching as long as there is . . .

"LIFE."

# FOURTEEN

## *IT IS WRITTEN*

In moving through life many of us are trying to connect with the Light of Life, but oftentimes we miss the connection. What we end up doing is amusing God.

Yes, it amuses Him as He observes the human in his efforts to explain Him. Ever since spirit was enrobed in the matter of a human, it has found itself entangled in the human ego. The human ego that is beset with the thought that it is up to it to explain God. The ego that dares, the man that follows its dictates.

Man has written the words . . .

Man has preached the words . . .

Man has ascribed the words . . .

He has made it his business to tell all fellowmen what God has supposedly said, what God meant by his words, who God really is, how God operates, and what His plans are. A comedy, produced by the human, and seen by God as pure entertainment. Reminds one of all those commentators who pop on television to explain what the person meant who just made a speech.

It would take many human life times to read all that man has written. It would take just as many to find the truth. Man has deemed his own words as that truth, as the only truth. Man has ignored the human behind the pen, he has ignored the fact that it was the perception of that human, it was speech by that human, and it was within the cycle of that human's life span.

God did not write anything. Never in the history of man has it been shown that God was the writer, that He was the author of anything.

God communicates, there isn't any question of that, but God does not bare His "soul" to man.

It is truly amazing that since man discovered "writing" he has embarked on this crusade to explain his Creator using the ability of creative writing that he received from the Creator.

Yes, as part of the race called human, this author could be similarly charged.

# FIFTEEN

## *IS IT BIRTH?*

This is life, it is movement, it is energy, it is action and it is eternal.

Mankind believes in a threshold, it believes it steps across it into another world. But what if man is really living life with one foot on each side of that threshold. Man lives the human life as spirit enrobed in the physical, but spirit lives in both worlds, all dimensions, simultaneously. It never comes, it never goes, it is already, "There."

Many claim to have experienced a temporary leave taking, a tunnel is always mentioned. Could we relate this leaving via a tunnel to arriving via a tunnel? A tunnel that could be the birth canal?

The action taking place within both tunnels strangely similar. A tunnel, a trip, a noise, and then popping into the light. When spirit chooses to enrobe itself in the human persona it is born into the light. When spirit discards the robe it is once again born into the light.

Spirit is the chooser, it decides on its mission, but once born into this light, seldom does the human part of spirit remember its trip. Neither is the mission remembered.

The world of spirit, the world of man?

Or . . . simply the same world viewed from a different angle?

# SIXTEEN

## *SPIRITUAL COMMUNICATION?*

Spirit moves through life, spirit lives in other worlds, in other dimensions. Since spirit theoretically is "free" who erects the barriers to completely free movement?

In this world spirit seems invisible to man, and yet spirit lives just as man does, so what prevents man from seeing it? Our world is referred to as a spiritual world, does this mean it's a world for the spirit and man is the intruder? The spirit world is a world full of activity, just as is the human world, but although the spirit can see both, man can only see his own.

From time to time, the human world seems to be able to take part in a spiritual communication. When man gets a message about a future event, who has decided to relay the information? There seems to be more of a sensing than an oral, and yet man seems to "hear" the words. Humankind, as a whole, does not seem to wish to open this door, is it missing an opportunity? Should it make more of an effort to communicate?

There were, and are, some in our society that have the ability, the talent, to have opened this door of communication. None probably to the degree that the man called, "The Sleeping Prophet" could. His name was Edgar Cayce, a wonder in the modern world. Cayce is long gone, but his work is carried forward by his family, although none seem to have inherited his extraordinary talent.

It is said that all humans have this talent, it lies dormant until something out of the ordinary happens or an individual makes it his business to pursue it.

Cayce certainly demonstrated that life goes on in this world and in the spiritual world. If he could communicate, if he could lie down and make contact with some unseen force, than it stands to reason there is something more beyond the senses of man. Could it be that what he tapped into was simply the wisdom of the universe?

Man is intrigued by the unexplainable, he is intrigued by a communication from the ether.

The years of change, the year 2000 and all those beyond it. We have seen what those in the past have wrought, will what is prophecized, will what is predicted carry similar weight? Communication taking place from both sides of the threshold as easily as a phone call is made? Communication from the other side, or that which was claimed to have been from there, shook up humanity in the past, will what is anticipated do the same? Modern man is looking for answers, he is turning inward hoping to find them. Can man find, within himself, the answer to what he seeks?

It is not easy to seek the knowledge that comes from within, it is even harder to get it from the world of spirit.

Man looks for an easy out, so if the inner search is too hard, and the world of spirit keeps the doors shut, he finds a human to focus on. He finds someone to put on a pedestal, to make him an icon, to listen to his preaching, and he overlooks the fact that this person is constructed of the same human matter he is, and is not endowed with any special qualities.

Why choose another human, why not look beyond him and choose the Creator? Why not make God the icon? Why not serve Him and not the human who only serves himself?

Spirit communication, is it with other spirits? Is it with the spirit of self? And why is it not with all spirits and not just the few? Is there a hierarchy in the spirit world that allows some to part the curtain at will, while others cannot?

Man is surrounded by spirit always, and it is the spirit that absorbs the personality it lives through as it moves through the human circle of life. It is the personality that transcends. Each personality added to spirit to become the sum total of all that we've been or will be. It is not spirit that is judged, it is the personality that moved through life during its time. It was this personality that made the choices, carried out its decisions, used its free-will.

Many refer to the spirit as the human spirit. The spirit is not human, never was never will be. It is the physical matter that it flows through that bears the nomenclature "human." This matter does not survive, only the personality it created does. We call it the "human" personality because we grow it as the result of our human actions.

When the personality transcends, when the spirit moves on, which does the communicating at the onset? Since there seems to be a holding area for a short time, which one does the communicating?

Some humans say they have developed the ability to channel spirits from beyond the threshold. But what if what is coming through is a personality that once was, and is still, encapsulated within their own spirit? It brings its own experience to the forefront of the mind of the one doing the channeling. It comes when summoned because it is already here, it does not come from another world because who it is, who it was, is contained for the moment in this particular human.

Could this be true of any spirit coming through to communicate? Is this why some are so knowledgeable, while others are not? Is this, as it is with any human? Not all are Nobel prize winners, not all use both oars when moving down the river of life.

When communication is established the communicant doesn't say much that would benefit mankind. Edgar Cayce could, and did, seem to reach a new plateau. He is gone and no one has been able to contact him for similar erudition.

What we can deduce, from the many communiqués, is that if a personality wasn't all that bright during its particular cycle, when it surfaces to make itself known, what will be brought forth will be just as mundane.

Why is it man cannot reach, cannot contact those who were scientists, inventors, doctors, philosophers, etc.? Those who made a difference while living in their moment of time? Is it because the spirits that contain these personalities are embedded in some humans in the now, and therefore cannot be reached? Their spirit embarked on a new cycle of learning, of growing a new personality?

Is this why those who channel, those who evoke the spirits seem limited in who they can reach? Or is there a dimension, a level that prevents penetration?

Man's spirit is comprised of many personalities. It is said these personalities are all around us, but in a dimension just beyond our own. It is also said that there are many dimensions and the spirit must work its way up to each new level. So are the spirits we reach only on the first level, the dimension that is just beyond our own? While those we can't reach are in other dimensions, on other levels, that preclude another human existence or an appearance?

Our civilization has made enormous strides, it has penetrated a world that is just barely out of reach. It is a spiritual world lived in by spirit at the same time it has one foot in the human world.

Man can make contact because a total crossover to another dimension has not been made as yet. Man is trying to learn all about it, spirit is trying to communicate. Sometimes there is a connection and when this happens man should be thankful, he has again been given a gift. He has been allowed to peek into his own past and his own future, even as he lives within this moment, this movement in time.

# SEVENTEEN

## *THE SPIRIT GIFT*

The movement of life, one of life's greatest mysteries. It encompasses so much, the mind has a hard time grasping it.

Spirit in this world, spirit in the next world, spirit eternal.

Although the idea seems far-fetched, although many choose not to accept it, the world of spirit is not a world out of sight, out of mind. It may seem to be a world beyond the senses of man and yet it manages to enter the sense world of man.

Many have heard that whisper in the ear.

Many have had that intuitive thought.

Many have been brave enough to admit it. Whether man wishes to admit it or not, such a communiqué is not as rare as some would have it. And yet when someone steps forth to speak about it he is labeled a kook. The standard response by those who refuse to admit there is more to the movement of life than what is seen. Edison could be called a kook, so could Copernicus, so could many others who had the courage to move with their dreams, and as a result the world has benefited.

Many, however, would rather not face this world of the unknown, it frightens them. And yet the world of the unknown is a much vaster place than the world of the known. The world of the unknown, the world of life out of time, the human himself. Who has any knowledge of what these really consist of? We pose a reality, but in fact we do not really know what "reality" is.

In fact, man lives his life in the unknown. Every day, every night, he takes part in living in a world he knows nothing about. Man does not even know what the next second, the next minute, the next hour, will bring. And yet he isn't bothered because he does not know. He continues his headlong rush as he moves through life.

When he retires at night, when he hops into bed he welcomes sleep. Does he give any thought to the fact that he is entering an unknown? Does he even know where spirit goes while he is sleeping? Life is moving whether he is awake or asleep. It is life in action, it is part of his life.

So the unknown is not a threat, neither are the messages received on the wind. All just a part of life, not only mortal life, but spiritual life. E-mail being sent by ancestors, by teachers, messengers all.

Receiving messages from the spirit to the spirit is nothing new. It is as old as man. It is the eternal life force at work.

Man is the human, it is spirit that is the energy, that is the soul.

Many books have been written, they attempt to define man. They call man a human entity. That he is. Some call him a human spirit, a human soul, man is the physical body, he is the human of the body. However, the soul, the spirit, are not human. Man can no more step across that threshold intact than he can fly (sans plane), but the soul, the spirit can step across with equanimity. They and man are not traveling companions. The personality that does the growing, while with man, moves forward while the physical becomes dust.

Man is capable of receiving messages from the world outside his vision. Spirit does speak to spirit. Man can also choose to accept or to ignore, he has his free-will. He may receive messages that seem beyond his control, but he does not need to follow their dictates.

The spirit in the next dimension can see much farther than the spirit in this dimension. It is not hampered by the physical. Does such a spirit believe it is its duty to pass on what it sees?

It is called the world of the psychic, it is a world of perception. Those who have the gift, have utilized a talent most unusual. They have opened themselves up to it, they have not closed the door. Fear closes the door, curiosity helps it to open.

The choice to accept allows the spirit entry, it allows the subconscious to receive a message, it allows the mind to process it, and it is proof positive that spirit lives on.

# EIGHTEEN

## THE VOICES ON THE WIND

As we move through life, messengers come to us along the way. They speak, they would relay a message, but man is too busy to listen, so the messengers go away, maybe next time . . .

Man says he seeks the truth, the truth that will explain mankind, and the truth that will direct mankind. However, when the messengers of truth appear, speak, man hears nothing. He is tuned out and not tuned in. The sense of inner hearing has deserted him.

There is a saying, "When the pupil is ready, the teacher will come." Well, it seems in the world of today, the teacher is ready, but the pupil is in limbo.

Ancient man lived by his senses, and he made the effort to listen in the quiet of inner self to the messages he received. The messages as conveyed by spirit to spirit. Ancient man was not as enthralled by his physical body as man is today. Modern man is so busy tending to the physical, that is only of a temporary nature, that he is ignoring his true spirit.

The physical does not progress spirit, only the self can progress spirit.

Why is man so lacking in awareness? What is it that leaves him so deficient in understanding?

Man was not born yesterday, if one uses the rules of time today, but he finds it extremely difficult to understand the messages that the messengers have brought him throughout his lifetime. The insight of illumination for him is merely a dim bulb.

The movement of life is not just for the now, it is eternal. It flows through the human, it flows through the spirit. Man has chosen not to put his belief in this, he has chosen to believe in the physical "I" of today.

Every religion, that is in the forefront today, has attributed its rise to a specific messenger. They came and they relayed what man was supposed to know, to learn, and then were gone. It seems man has a memory problem and no sooner does the messenger go away then man starts to forget. It has happened throughout the millennias, man is retentive memory challenged.

Chicken Little running around clucking, "The sky is falling," had nothing on man who is fixated on the idea the world is about to end.

If man stopped to analyze this idea he would realize that the concept of the world coming to an end is simply in context to what will happen to him. Yes, the world will end, but it will be his own world, the world of his physical matter. Man is merely viewing the end of the world from a fallacious perspective.

Man has also put his faith, not in his Creator, but in the scientific world. It has generated more wordage, numbers, analyses, about this planet, all planets, the universe, space, what have you, and has come to the conclusion it has all the answers. It knows how all began, it knows how all will end. It seeks to explain space and all in it, but it has yet to decide the dimensions of space. As for the universe, the universes, it believes it has the definitive answers, today, only to find it must backtrack tomorrow.

But what is it science keeps overlooking, what is it forgetting to put into its analytical equations? Simple!
But for the Creator who created all . . .
But for the Creator who created man . . .
But for the Creator who gave man a mind, a brain . . .
There would not be anything, especially the field of science.

Science will continue to discover only what it will be allowed to discover. The brain is finite, the mind is infinite and as such its capabilities beyond the scope of science.

Man may have been given will power, free will, choice, dominion over much, but he was never granted dominion over universal mind, nor what he refers to as "his" mind.

Man is not a Johnny-come-lately to this planet, nor to many others and yet the universes out there are beyond his scope, even beyond his imagination. The Age of Man would better be referred to as the Ages of Man. He's been, he's gone, he comes again. Sometimes brilliant, sometimes not so. He creates for his time and moves on. Each time he comes he experiences, he learns, but only to the ability he has at the time to comprehend. What he seems to find the hardest to learn, to comprehend, is his own spirit and the truth within that spirit.

As man does his learning on earth in stages, so also does spirit in the eternal world of spirit.

Man learns during his "life" time. Spirit learns during its eternality. The school of "life" never shuts its doors. And as with the school during the life of physical matter, the eternal one is also graded. "Life" as it is lived in matter is judged when it dispenses with matter.

Man finds it difficult to learn responsibility, and when he is made to "pay" for his action he goes into a blame mode. He blames everyone, but the self, the one who instigated the action. What "one" does, does come back to "haunt" one.

The river flows to the sea . . .

The spirit keeps moving . . .

Man will follow the movement of life . . .

Man must follow his conscience . . .

Man must follow spirit . . .

And man must not continue to close his eyes to the truth when it is revealed by the messenger.

It is the truth that will set all mankind free.

Spirit, freed from the shackles of the physical, will return home.

Insight, illumination, revelation, all contained in one word . . . TRUTH.

The messengers are sent to remind man that it is not man's world, it is God's world, and it is He who will decide what to do with it.

# NINETEEN

## A "NEW" AGE?

Moving through life is living life through the stages that are inherent in it, but also through the stages man sets.

Before man considered himself civilized, before he created a society, a culture, he was already moving through life, and living it. Whatever occurs as a result of man's actions is not a phenomenon, it is merely a progressive step forward in his own development.

Some, today, scoff at what they call the New Age Adherents. They do not miss an opportunity to laugh, to bash, to sneer, at everything different that is being attributed to the "New Agers." The key word is, "different." They do not understand so they label all that transpires as weird. However, when one stops to think about it, hasn't there always been a "New Age?"

The origin of the earth . . . New Age.
The origin of man . . . New Age.
The beginning of religion . . . New Age.
The progression of man . . . New Age.
The civilization of man . . . New Age.
The socialization of man . . . New Age.
The culturization of man . . . New Age.

We could say a "New Age" begins every time a child is born, no child is ever born into an "Old Age."

So a "New Age" is always in the process of being.

What we believe, how we believe contributes to that label "New" while others would call it the "World of Merlin." New anything is not sinister, it is simply man turning his think around. Whether it be looking at those around him in a new way, paying attention to the health of one's body, trying to make a societal, a cultural change or even by the use of technology, and moving it out into space. As man thinks, so he is, and nothing is new, it is only the other side of the same coin.

There is always a new millennia, it is man's time moving in time with the steps of life. He has made the journey many times and each cycle has been a new cycle, a New Age. His racial memory usually brings to the forefront something from his dim past and he sets about giving it reality again.

So many would deride those who would get together in what is called a "Harmonic Convergence." New? New Age? Why would they think so? It has probably happened many times before. The heads on Easter Island, the stones we see arranged in such symmetrical circles all over the world, the age-old temples, etc. Man must have converged many times, he was simply trying to get in harmony with himself, as well as his world.

Crystals? What is wrong with associating them with many of man's actions? They are not a New Age phenomenon, they are as old as man and have already had a place before in his life.

Man as a dreamer, an illusionist, a thinker. He attempts to create a reality to who he is by trying to look at both sides of his moving life. Man sees what he wishes to see, while he rides that escalator of life.

Man has been riding this escalator for eons, man has created his beliefs at each stage of the ride. To say what he believes today is myth, is to forget that spirit rides with man, and spirit is not a myth.

What is revolutionary philosophic think today, has its roots in racial memory.

What is revolutionary philosophic think today, is fact tomorrow.

New Age becomes Old Age only to become New Age again. It is a cycle.

# TWENTY

## *THE FUTURE THAT WILL JUDGE US*

Will those who come after us in the millennia ahead use time as we know it today, or will they scoff at our naiveté?

No doubt they will. Not having lived in the past, not knowing anything about the past, man tends to look at it as an old fuzzy, jerky, movie. All happening on a screen, having nothing to do with his reality.

But man lives his life, day to day, in the time of his life. His present is real to him, his past is dim to him, his future is unknown to him. No one can look back and give validity to events that took place in the times of a "then," just as no one can look ahead and give validity to future events. So to say, it happened, it will happen, is simply the thought process at work in the now. And thought is an anomaly.

So, how can we give credence to predictions put forth by prophets? Judiciously, but also with the knowledge that thought comes from within, spirit lives within, and we haven't a clue as to how it moves us. We must hear the words from those who voice them and sift through them looking for that mustard seed.

As civilized as man thinks he is, he does not have a clue as to how the world of spirit works. Spirit is not a part of civilization, of society, of culture, or anything of a human nature.

Man lives, man dies, so has been written, but if man believes in his spirit, he knows there isn't any "death." Spirit has eternal life and spirit does not step over any threshold, neither does man.

Man prides himself on his technology of today, he overlooks the source of that technology. It came through mind and it came through mind for the use of the human today.

Technology from the mind, but not a "human" mind.

A future looking back at its past and seeing . . . us.

Has any one given any thought to the idea that the "future" could already be looking back at us? If it takes light millions of years to reach the earth from those far distant recesses, could it be said that the future is already judging us?

Since spirit does not die, could it be riding that beam of light heading our way? Spirit is not hampered by time, since in the world of spirit, time does not exist.

# TWENTY-ONE

## *WHO ARE WE?*

Life moves, but it doesn't move in any particular direction.

We assume it is a linear one. From alpha to omega, from beginning to end, from birth to death. This is how man views it. Life does not have a form, and life does not have a direction. It moves and yet it stands still. Life is not only a phenomenon, it is an anomaly. The only one who knows what it is all about is the One who created it.

Man who seeks to duplicate the function, to clone it, finds he is unable to do so past a certain point. Inevitably he must make use of a portion of the original seed. The seed that rebirths itself. The spiritual seed that is not only for this time, but is also for no-time, as well.

It seems that when man addresses the subject of reincarnation as a continuing life force, a life movement, what is promoted the most is a return of the self. The La Brea Tar Pits couldn't be murkier! What is it that returns? Is it the same spirit with a new guise? The same spirit with a new self?

If the meaning of reincarnation is the return of the same self, what does this do to the theory some hold that they come back using the persona of different members of the family they were once a part of?

And if man feels his spirit of today, will return as his Father, Mother, whatever, tomorrow, then man has created an anomaly of spirit.

The return of spirit as a continuing life flow is not one that is in doubt, rising as a myriad of spirits raises questions.

If we follow the thread of the spirit that is in the human and see it as reincarnating itself within a certain human group simply because it is atoning for a previous wrong to a member within that group, we could conclude that in all of life their is only one spirit.

God creating Adam as one spirit, then creating Eve as the same spirit. Adam and Eve, their children, the same spirit. One spirit, split like an atom into many pieces, but still only one spirit?

We never become individuals, we never have our own spirit, we are merely many "selves" within one? We are an illusion, a dream?

What are we to think about the theory that we are here to perfect the self, perfect the spirit, when we do not have our own spirit?

I am you, you are me, we are us, we are one!

What you do effects me, what I do effects you.

If this were so, why were Adam and Eve instructed to go forth and multiply, why bother to create the human? If life was good in the Paradise of the spirits, the archangels, the angels, the cherubim and all those assorted tenants, why bother creating a human to gum up the works?

The concept of Paradise then needs to be questioned. Were all who dwelt there individual spirits, or only one spirit? The process that humans were endowed with to perpetuate themselves was it a similar process used in Paradise or was the spirit world static? Where then did all those occupants of Paradise come from?

Since life is eternal, why does there have to be the need for the human cycle? Many say to experience life, but aren't spirits already experiencing life?

We believe we are, we think we are, but what if we are not?

Real, that is?

La Brea Tar Pits or the Black Lagoon couldn't be any more murkier than this line of thought.

# TWENTY-TWO

## *ANOTHER ANOMALY?*

Is the planet earth we call home, another anomaly?
Many would like to believe that the earth and the humans who dwell on it are the only such in the entire universe.

If all held this belief, the next question should be, "Then why the need for the universe? Why all the other planets, why all that is out there?" We do not have an answer, but the reasoning process alone should tell us, we are only a minute portion of the movement called eternal life.

As man goes through his known human cycles on this planet, other unknown cycles are taking place in the universes. Maybe even out of time. Our time not being their time.

We could be an anomaly, we could be the only human occupied planet, we could be an experimental one. A creation, within a creation, within a creation, etc.

However, rationalization should qualify such thought. When we take the time to look around. When we take the time to look at the variety of what is called life just on this planet, it should give us pause. Why not life elsewhere?

When man thinks of eternal, he has a tendency to limit its parameters. Eternal means no parameters, it's an ad infinitum thing.

Man does not have the knowledge, man does not have the wisdom, he cannot visualize anything without a finite end. And man cannot visualize any life without humans in it, at least humans who resemble him.

Man endeavors to limit the movement of life, he tends to visualize a river's end, he puts a fence around what he calls his universe.

Man accepts the movement of life, but only within the parameters of his think.

# TWENTY-THREE

## THE SURF OF LIFE

The movement of life is reflected by the surf as it washes up on the beaches of life. The surf, as it moves willy-nilly, here and there, backward and forward, sliding under, crashing over, whatever lies in its path. Thought isn't any different.

Our universe evidently is a thinking one, and it reacts in much the same way as the thought of man. It has its moments of calmness, it has its moments of chaos. It has its moments of life and it has its moments of death. The universe of man, man in the universe, both reflections of each other, both establishing the parameters of the movement called life to suit their needs.

Man has the power to tap into the vault of the universe. He has the power to open the doors to avail himself of what it holds.

Man has been of two minds about this power. He seeks to fling open those doors and he seems reluctant at the same time.

We do not know how man utilized this power in the "time" of no-time. He could have availed himself of this knowledge. He could have tapped into the mysteries, and been able to zip around the galaxies with ease. We do not know if ancient man availed himself of universal wisdom, the time lapse is too great, but modern man is seeking to dip his toe into this unique surf.

Modern man says he is using his brain, but the brain is merely part of the physical of man. It is the motor. Modern man cannot rely on this motor if he seeks to move out into the universe, he must rely on his mind and must not limit its activity. Brain cannot expand, but mind knows no limits, no dimensions. If todays man seeks to tap into the mind of the universe he must use his mind to do it.

So as man today steps out to seek wisdom, to seek enlightenment, he must move mind to the forefront. Mind is not stagnant but it does need a push from man. Man must begin the action.

Lifetimes have come and gone, every one a wonderful time, but lifetimes are what man makes of them. Man can look at his past as part of history, his heritage, but when he does this he must not allow himself to stop at an imaginary line from his past. He cannot limit his think to, "The human began life . . . here." Because before "known man" there was life.

The universe is not a known, it is a mystery. It can teach us much, it can hide even more.

The spirit is a mystery, man is a mystery, trying to solve who we are is not an easy task, in fact it is an impossible one.

We seek enlightenment, but are we seeking it in all the wrong places?

No one person can teach us enlightenment. No one person can give us insight. No one person can give us light. Why? Because each and everyone of us must do it for ourselves. What we fail to realize is that we already have light, we are light, when we look into the mirror and into our own eyes we can see the light. We were born of the light.

The physical body each of us dons when we enter the cycle of life does not have any history. We create the history for the body. The body will reflect our lifestyle, but that lifestyle will not transcend.

Yes, every lifetime is a wonderful lifetime because spirit has chosen to live it in the physical.

We may be battered by the surf of life, we may rise and fall with the waves as they race for the shore, it is only part of the enlightenment process.

Living life, experiencing life, moving through life, eventually brings us to the time when we must enter the tunnel. The matter is discarded as we enter the tunnel and we emerge as pure spirit.

Is it then we achieve enlightenment?

# TWENTY-FOUR

## *LIGHTING THE BULB*

Can man, in his pursuit of the inner self, eliminate a few steps on his way to enlightenment? More so, can he skip over a few planes, eliminate a few dimensions? Can man affect his destiny by shortening his spiritual path? And how long is that path anyway? Can man transcend time and thought and bring himself closer to the light? Or is "man" out of the loop?

Higher conscience, we hear so much about it. Does conscience really have lower and higher properties? Isn't the conscience supposed to be a pure essence within man? When we go into the inner self isn't it the conscience we wish to contact?

Man speaks quite glibly about this part of the self. He defines it to encompass what he perceives it to be.

Is there any human on this planet that has found enlightenment? That has the knowledge to define, to explain, the unseen? When man seeks to expand his consciousness, how does he set out to do it? It seems man has given form to something that doesn't have a form.

We experience the lessons of life through our senses. The senses do not have form. They are as undefined as is the conscience. Are they part of it? Or are they merely a faculty for the use of the human? Surely, the spirit does not need the senses? To smell, too hear, to talk, to feel, to see, all this action depends on something that is part of the human body. When this matter is no longer, neither are the senses.

Science has cut up man, "Six ways from Sunday." An expression that supposedly denotes everything has been covered. What science has not found is what gives man his uniqueness. It has not found conscience, it has not found spirit, it has not found soul, it has not found the senses. Science has found the mechanics behind the senses. It has not found anything it can see or touch that is not a part of the physical.

Science has found ways to transfer human body parts, but science has not found a way to transfer the intangibles. It can transfer "life," but only when using the seed that gives life. Science cannot transfer the energy called, "LIFE."

Salome danced behind seven veils, so it's been said, man lives life behind his own seven veils. Are they the seven veils to his past, his now, his future? Are they the seven veils he moves through on his way to the light?

Is it possible for man to look back, move aside a veil, and see who he was in a previous lifetime?

Is it possible for "man" to step across the threshold, pull aside a veil and see what is in store for him on another level?

Many in our society believe that they step back in time as they attempt to regress. Are they seeing a past reality or is mind creating a scenario for them. Are they producing a film of wishful thinking? Man's mind can produce, can create, can visualize any scenario man wishes.

Stepping across the threshold used to be a one-way trip. Nowadays so many seem to be able to purchase round trip tickets that it makes one wonder. Are they really pushing aside the first veil? Are they really experiencing what they say they are? Or is mind again at work, directing, producing, displaying, an illusion, a holograph?

Does one's conscience remain with the spirit throughout eternity? Or does each being arrive with a new one at birth?

Have those who speak of all these matters with such authority given all of us a false impression?

Seeking within the self in order to manifest one's hopes, dreams, desires, is nothing new. Man has had this ability, this talent, ever since he became man. Man's history will bear this out.

Looking into the inner for the answers, will provide man with a very important one. He asks, and invariable, he learns, "He is complete." Nothing more can be given, nothing can be taken away. He need not conduct all the searches to find what he believes is missing. It is all there. Now all man must do is use what he has as he lives life through his created energy.

It has been said that man can manifest anything he wishes into his life in the same way he has manifested self. If we look around our planet, the credibility of this statement should not be in any doubt. The stamp of man's work is everywhere. The "I am" of man, and the "I can" of man giving credence to each other. Will power and choice the means of action.

In the world of today, with so many claiming themselves as victims and blaming all and sundry for whatever situation befalls them, it certainly would be of benefit to them to break this chain of thought. They would be enlightened by the results.

All can find enlightenment, all can see the light, all is up to the self of today. The self of the conscience.

The "Source" looks at man and says, "What in the world is your problem? I gave you everything and you have failed to use it all. You have decided to limit yourself to ten percent and allowed ninety percent to lie fallow. You cannot grow anything on fallow soil. You must plant the seed, you must water it, you must nurture it. To you all has been given, why aren't you taking advantage of it?"

The light bulb that just went on . . . was it enlightenment or was it only knowledge?

# TWENTY-FIVE

## *WHY DO WE FORGET?*

We move through life like beginners, from lifetime to lifetime, completely forgetting that we have been here before. So each time we pick a new life, we start from the beginning, is it any wonder we do not seem to be getting anywhere? The human life seems to be a seeking life, and each time man is left wanting.

The philosophies are varied, man is unsure which to embrace, so he moves from one to another, but spirit is never satisfied. It searches for peace for the self, and it eludes it. He never seems to awaken the racial memory sufficiently before it is again time to leave. The eternal treadmill keeps moving.

What is man to do? How can he move beyond the treadmill? How can he attain what he seeks in the now of his today? Man is the "I" of today and he is the ego of that I. Man has allowed it to dictate what it wants, what it desires, overlooking the needs of the "I" that is also of the spirit. Man must move his ego from the primary position within and place the I of the spirit in that place.

If one looks carefully at the concept of ego, one will find it is the ego that runs this world, and it is man who obeys its dictates. It makes man's bed and man lies in it, completely ignoring the fact that this is not how things are meant to be.

What would happen if man set about reversing this happenstance? Wouldn't his life change? Would not the realization come to him that he is in the world on a temporary basis? And everything in this world is of a temporary nature? Would his values change? Ego has values of its own construct and these are not the values endorsed by spirit.

Man is always in search of heaven. He expects to go there when his time is up. Ask him to describe heaven and he describes all the things he would love to have while living this life. Has he described heaven? Hardly! He has described only his perception of what he would like it to be.

Man keeps looking for the Kingdom of Heaven someplace in the stratosphere. What makes him think it is above him? Has he forgotten the words, "The Kingdom of God lies within?" Heaven, neither up nor down, but within, and always with him.

When man sets out to look for heaven he forgets to look within the self.

Man arrives, man leaves, but the self of the I that is, never goes, never comes, it always is.

The end without a beginning.

The beginning without an end.

# TWENTY-SIX

## *FOOLISH MAN*

Man has a saying, "The future is in the hands of man." This is a spurious saying because the future definitely is not in the hands of man, it is in the "hands" of God.

Man moves through life, but he is not in control of "LIFE." Man is or should be, in control of self, his conduct. In the world of today man has chosen to ignore this truism and society is suffering.

There are very few truths in the life of man . . .

One seems to be that he must suffer. Suffering is tied in with daily existence.

Two is that he is in constant search of fulfillment. He is always desiring something.

Three would seem to be if he eliminated desire, he would eliminate suffering.

Four, the essence of which is, that man can eliminate desire by living life with exemplary conduct.

Man comes full circle when he embarks on a search for truth.

Society seems to have abandoned the path to self-realization and instead has chosen the path of catering to the ego, not to the self of spirit, but the self of ego.

Man feels he need not consider fellow man as he goes through this life. He has put aside the understanding of what is right and what is wrong, and the media of today is filled with deeds that are certainly not meritorious.

It seems as one wades through the history of man, that every couple of thousand years or so, someone is born to again show man the path to perfecting the self. Man watches, man listens, and before long man ignores what was said and seen, and once again steps off the path of rectitude. Man finds the new path more pleasurable and easier to follow. It is his "now" path and he is not in any hurry to follow his spiritual path.

Is it any wonder that man's quest for enlightenment, for insight, has such an uphill climb? Man continually abandons his basic faith to follow the will-o-the-wisp called ego. And to follow ego is like trying to walk the spiritual path backwards.

In man's search for meaning to his life, in his search for his basic values, he overlooks several more truths . . .

He is here, he was born.

He will leave this place because he must die.

Between one and the other he has a golden opportunity.

He can spend the time satisfying his ego or he can spend the time perfecting the self.

Man has always been given a choice, he has yet to make the right decision.

# TWENTY-SEVEN

## *THE MATURATION FLOW*

Man moves through life, but his growth, his maturation as a spirit, seem to be hindered by the robes of the human. Man fails to apply himself with any diligence.

Why does man not value "life" as he should? He has been given something precious, a rare gem, and he does not see or appreciate the value.

Man establishes his patterns early in life and as he moves through it, loathes to give them up. He attaches to them like a magnet.

If man wishes to grow, to mature in spirit, he must not cling to attachments that prevent him from moving forward. If man lives his present with equanimity, his future will reflect it. If he does nothing, he will still move forward and his future will also reflect this nothingness.

Man's life is his dream, and his dream is his life. He is experiencing inwardly what he seeks to experience outwardly, and he experiences outwardly what is occurring inwardly.

Life does not stand still, it is movement, and the movement is one of constant change. Moment to moment, it flows through man, man cannot stop it.

Bodily changes occur, mind changes occur, man believes he is in control and finds that life pays no attention to what he thinks.

If man would take each moment as it occurs and try to analyze it, he would find it gone before the thought was completed.

But man can grow, he can mature, even though he finds life's movements are beyond his control. If he looks to his spirit, lives his life according to his conscience, he will find that as each moment is ticked off he has added to the self, he has gained maturation.

Mind flows, breath flows, energy flows, life flows.

# TWENTY-EIGHT

## *THE MOVEMENT WITHOUT END*

The movement of life takes place throughout our entire planet, our universe. No one part of the world, no human throughout the world, can claim exclusivity or knowledge about this movement.

Within the movement some strange things occur and man becomes privy to some of them. The mind easily makes the trip, but the human finds it difficult to make the journey. He is held back by the form of his humanness.

Man is also held back by the knowledge he acquires because he associates knowledge with wisdom and that is far from the truth.

Man has a tendency to talk about miracles, miraculous events, phenomenon, stuff he has a problem understanding. Are such things real or is the movement of mind a deceiver? Skeptics doubt when one individual claims to see, to hear, but what about those doubts when many see?

The movement of life is the movement of the unknown.

Man would define this movement, he would give it parameters, but no matter what he does it is still an unknown.

Is the movement of life taking place simultaneously? Is the past, the now, the future, all taking place in the movement of the breath of the moment? If this is so, how then can man try to define it using such terms as past, present, future?

The movement of life an unknown, and yet it can be described as a miracle, a phenomenon.

What is a miracle, what is a psychic, what is a mystic?

A miracle is defined as a wonder; a supernatural happening.

A psychic is defined as a spiritualist.

A mystic is defined as applying to secret religious rites; to mysticism; to a mystery.

Not great definitions or satisfactory explanations. It seems when one deals with the unknown that is what it is . . . unknown. And those who would peer into the depths have chosen to use a gift they hope will enable them to penetrate the murk. They seek to define the movement of life.

Man has traveled the world in search of such phenomenon. What he has learned makes science-fiction look tame by comparison.

In Tibet, we still find many who are called mystics. We find psychics in all four corners of this world. Miracles are said to be taking place everywhere.

What causes all this? Some explain it as mind being used to concentrate with such intensity that currents of energy begin to flow in all directions. The flow attracts the "matter" that is all around, like a magnet. The same waves that enable our radios and our TV's to work.

Whether it is a miracle, whether it's a psychic at work, whether it's a mystic seeking a message, "communication" is taking place.

Communication that isn't any different than the movement of life. There is a flow and modern man has yet to uncover why or how such phenomenon occur.

Research to uncover the mechanism of this activity is taking place, once the mechanics are explained, will it still be a phenomenon?

Will the movement of life no longer be an unknown?

Man would like to believe he has found the key, but what he does not see is that he has not as yet found the door.

# TWENTY-NINE

## "LIGHT" AS SPIRIT?

The movement of life created by the Master of Life. Why does man continue to place Him in the position of assistant?

Man has created what he calls the "Holy Trinity." The Father, the Son, and the Holy Spirit . . . at least this is the structure as recognized by some religions. A corporation created with God being one-third of it. God is God . . . He is not one third of anything. Man, by placing Him in such a role, takes away from the Oneness of God. He demotes Him into a subservient position.

God stands alone. The Son may have come into being by the action of the Father, the Holy Ghost may have been created by the Father, but neither is the Father. There is but one "Light" and mankind is part of it. All are specks of light, of life, from the one "Light."

Should man, as part of his religious belief, elevate the Son, elevate the Ghost, and put them on a par with God? God was not born of man.

All peoples believe in a Spirit, their nomenclature for this Spirit as varied as their culture, their religious belief. The Christians created a Trinity to worship.

Belief originates in man, to question that belief is not to denigrate it, but to challenge. No religious group should denounce the belief of its fellow man, but it can challenge a presumption created for man, by man. The belief may be challenged but the faith behind it is part of the structure of man. Belief has a time span, faith is eternal.

It's been said that the Apostles of the Bible carried on the work of the Holy Spirit, but wasn't it simply working for God, through their own spirit?

It has always been difficult to explain the lack of understanding, the confusion, that man has heaped on himself as he establishes his "beliefs." And how diversified those beliefs have become.

Truth, error, unbelief, belief. Choices made by the human who is of the God who gave him life. The same God who urges each human to believe in Him, whatever the nomenclature used.

To even think, to even say, that God prefers one religion over another is to denigrate God. God did not invent religion. He does not give any human, or any religious group, special preference because of its belief. How we live the life given us is our choice. God will not interfere in our choices or in how we demonstrate our beliefs. A belief can lead one down many paths, none any higher than the next, but it is the faith brought forth from one's inner depths that guides, that leads, that knows the way. When man crosses that invisible threshold, he does not cross it as a representative of any religious group, he simply steps over as the eternal spirit he is.

Yes, the Apostles preached, yes those who represented other religions did the same, they were spreading their belief. But as men born of man, it was the belief of man and they had an agenda. So it is with all men who set out to preach, to promulgate a belief.

Before the words of some 2000 years ago were anointed as Gospel, there had been many other words. Words that reached far back to a time before time. They were spoken, also as a Gospel; they were said to be right; they were said to be true, but they also came from the lips of man. God heard, God saw, but even then He did not interfere, He did not deny man his choice, He did not take away his free-will to believe as he chose to.

From his very beginning man has been doing the speaking, the interpreting. It is man who believes he has the answers. But when man leaves behind the robe of matter, and is simply spirit, he realizes that he needed nothing only the faith he was born with, as he moved through life.

Faith in his own spirit, the spirit born of truth.

Faith in the One who gave him life.

Faith in the "Light" of eternality.

# THIRTY

## *MAN OR SPIRIT?*

Following the spirit in the spirituality called, "New." A tangent or simply a natural step as one moves forward seeking enlightenment?

Man is being shown a new way, a new approach. He has knocked on the door and it is slowly opening. What now? Will man step back and allow it to close again as he holds on to what is familiar?

Man claims to be searching for something more in his life, but when given the opportunity he hesitates. To, "boldly go forward, where no man has been," is to step through that door.

Man says he is seeking in order to expand his "conscience." This is man's perspective of it. Man seems to feel he must become mentally awake to his surroundings, a laudable goal. But if man seeks to expand his "conscience" he should be aware that it doesn't need expanding, it is as wholly encompassing as it was when first given him. It is a conscience without parameters. What man fails to consider is that it has been he who has set the limits to understanding.

Out "there" is space eternal, without any edges, boundaries, parameters.

In "here" is conscience, it also is eternal, without any edges, boundaries, parameters.

To man has been given, it is his choice, his decision, what he decides to use.

Man moves through his life, through its ups and downs, and when things aren't to his liking or life seems overwhelming, he turns to God to ask for help, to demand help.

Man believes God is there at his beck and call. What man has decided to forget is that while in spirit, before his spirit enrobed itself in the matter man is today, "it" had been allowed to choose.

God allowed spirit to make a choice to enable it to experience life as a human. To experience all the ups, all the downs, of choice, of free-will. Spirit was given a choice of body, spirit was given a choice of experience. Spirit knew that as it moved through the human life it would be moving closer to the perfection which is its ultimate goal, it would be earning credits, points.

Man has suffered a racial memory loss. God will not step in and hold his hand every time he cries for help. God bestowed on him will-power and choice. Whatever occurs in his life is by his choice, however convoluted it seems. A choice was made before spirit garbed itself in matter and choices continue to be made while spirit is within matter. This was a chosen "cross" to bear.

Spirit, in moving through life within a human, is aware of the many leaders, of the many religions. Each one trying to explain God to him; each one trying to inform him what God means; each one putting words in God's "mouth" and then moving on to interpret those words.

The spirit, in its dual role, as spirit eternal, and as the "I" that lives today, certainly must find the situation a learning experience.

The spirit, that truly knows its origin, steps to one side, while the "I" of today listens to all the words uttered by fellow man and believes they are the truth. The spirit has been there, man merely guesses, theorizes. Spirit knows, man does not.

If man would simply listen to the spirit of his "conscience," and not to fellow man, the door that is slowly creaking open, would swing wide.

Man would find insight, man would find enlightenment, man would realize that spirit knows the way and is willing to lead man along the true path.

# THIRTY-ONE

## *REALITY?*

Moving through the present, the now, the today, isn't any different than it ever was. Time hasn't any meaning and man creates his own reality.

Man tries to step back in time to his past, drag it into today and he then says this is reality, this is valid. Is it? After all, the past is no longer here, so how can it be real? Man can only give a type of reality to what occurs in the now of his eye-blink. The blink comes, it goes, and whatever occurred is now the past.

Man cannot blink himself into the future, either. This is such an ephemeral state that man cannot give it form or make it a reality.

Man cannot seek to commit himself to any religion. Religion is an organized structure of man and it is not a Utopia for him to lose himself in. Just as man is a temporary being, so is the religion he espouses. Both are only for the "now."

Man must keep in mind the now is a construct without time. While he is moving through his now, he must see himself as moving through it as spirit. The "I" that is the physical matter of today must be taught to listen to spirit and not to all the rhetoric of man.

If man knew who he was, he would no longer seek.

If man would stop being so enamored with his own rhetoric he would be able to strip it to its basics.

If man stopped trying to run the life of his fellow man he might be able to see his own needs.

And no one can do this for the "I" of today, only the eternal spirit.

That is "reality!"

# THIRTY-TWO

## *THE LEARNING CYCLE*

We move through life as if in a dream, do we give reality to the dream? It has been said that the movement of life through man's life is a construct of his own creation. It is he who gives the "reality" to his illusions.

Man moves through life on a worldly level and he moves through life on a spiritual level.

He has been told, by fellow man, that he is here to demonstrate love, compassion, kindness. But this is fellow man speaking and God did not confide in him any specifics in his role as a human. Man, as usual, jumps to conclusions. So he looks for Paradise but only finds a fool's Paradise.

Love, compassion, kindness, are certainly part of his humanity, but humanity is not a one-sided role. Man is here to experience, to learn, all that life in the physical has to offer. He is here to learn the good, experience the bad, and take in the lessons of both. He starts below the first rung of the ladder and moves upward, a rung at a time. Each rung adds to this experience of the self. And each rung could be a cycle of human life.

Man is constantly being tested, if he were not, how else would he know what he has learned or not learned?

The gifts man has been given, besides the one of life in a

physical form, are many. Will-power, choice, talents beyond counting, were not given because they translated into love, compassion, kindness. They were given as tools for action. The action of choosing how to live this life, the action of will power to decide whether one could avoid the pitfalls or whether one simply fell into them. The action of choosing to be compassionate, to love, to demonstrate kindness.

As we look around our planet today, we find that many have chosen not to demonstrate the action that results in love, compassion, kindness.

If man arrived with love, kindness, compassion, etc., why would the trip be necessary? He would have already attained the goal of perfection.

Man's movement through life would not be very productive if, like a rolling stone, he gathered no moss. Or if it were like the river with barely a trickle of water in it. So man's movement goes through many phases. Stormy, restful, moving with speed, and idling in place. He is experiencing, he is taking his lessons to heart. He is moving up the rungs of the ladder, and when he is ready to step off the top rung he'll be ready to answer the question that will be posed to his spirit, "What did you learn about life while living it as a human?"

# THIRTY-THREE

## *LOOKING BACK AT THE FUTURE*

So what has man learned? Moving through life exposes the weird side of life. We read, we hear, about the many happenings that cannot be explained satifactorily. The field of the paranormal can be viewed as abnormal.

There have always been pyschics, mediums, seers, etc. Some seem to use the gift given them in a responsible manner, others do not.

We tend to our world, our universe, our space. We erect a barrier and do not allow ourselves to penetrate this barrier. The barrier, at times, seems to begin at the very tip of our noses. The barrier is akin to the flat-earth theory held by so many in a past that was only yesterday.

Man in moving through life must keep himself open to all it has to offer. A closed mind is not a progressive mind, but an open mind must also be selective in what it chooses to believe, so a judicious caution is a necessity.

The phenomenon of seeing beyond the immediate senses into a world not affected by space, by time, is to tap into a force beyond any explanation.

Some in our world today seem to be able to do it with ease. All mankind has the ability, but only a few choose to make use of it.

Precognition is stepping across a time barrrier into the future, but is it really the future? If all life happens in cycles and is only of the moment, could those who manage to see past the curtain, merely be tapping into universal mind? Do they see what has already taken place, a rerun of sorts?

Today our intent is to recycle the products used in daily life, could we also be recycling thoughts, events, happenings? After all isn't the human a recycled being? The matter decomposed into the earth, the spirit recycled into new matter?

We've had seers, in the past, who have spoken of what was not even part of their life at the time. They spoke of atom bombs, of airplanes, of submarines. How could they have seen things that were not to be invented for hundreds of years? Is all that ever was, ever will be, already present in universal mind? The mind without a beginning, without an end, man allowing the mind of self to make the journey and return with a thought, a picture, an idea, from the storehouse of universal mind?

Man tends to view his past and his future as separate events. He looks at his past as a record of himself, he looks at his future as yet to be, so to him it is not real because he cannot visualize it. However, this is man's thought process at work reasoning out something that to him is unknown. But the future is already out there, it is merely waiting for man to catch up. Like the light waves from that someplace in space. They are a past, since they began their journey thousands and thousands of years ago, and they are the future because it will be as many thousands of years before they reach their destination. But they are already fact, a reality.

The movement of life is an ongoing one. Time does not exist for the movement. Man can stand at the peak of his current existence and see the past, the present, the future.

But man must be willing to embrace the sense that lies be-yond the five he is so familiar with.

Should man refer to it as ESP (extrasensory perception)?

Should man refer to it as precognition?

Should man refer to it as paranormal?

Or should man recognize it for what it really is, the move-ment of life being recycled courtesy of the unversal mind?

The future already is the past.

# THIRTY-FOUR

## *CAN WE "SEE" LIFE?*

The movement of life continues even though it cannot be observed. The movement of life is represented by energy and energy cannot disappear, cannot be dispelled. It remains in the atmosphere, and it is not bound by time or dimension.

Man is comprised of energy, whether the energy is his spirit, his soul, has not been determined, but it has the same eternality.

Spirit was, spirit is, spirit will be, and man may view its function, its activities, its actions, as a part of the paranormal. The truth is . . . it is entirely normal! The explanation, the difference, only in the eyes of the human.

Man, through the sense beyond the five senses, can get in touch with past energies. They are all around him, the levels, the dimensions, not to be touched, not always seen, but there just the same.

When will man admit that there is a world he cannot explain away with any theories propounded by the scientific world. The world of science is a self-limiting one. The light bulb is still in the dim mode.

Many books have been written, many words have been spoken, and man continues to doubt the existence of this unseen world or worlds, as well as the energy that flows in and out. The only explanation, the only reason that man does not open his eyes so he can really "see," is because he is afraid.

He's been taught that when human matter is no more "life" ceases. He has lived his life accordingly, sometimes responsibly, most of the time irresponsibly. If man allowed the fact to penetrate that all his life he's been taught a lie, what would happen?

Would man change his way of living?

Would he become more aware of the consequence of his actions?

Would he accept complete responsibility for the energy he actually is?

Would the fact that he is under observation at all times cause him to think twice before doing someone an injustice? Man is observed, but his actions aren't interfered with because he is here to learn his lessons, to experience "life."

One could cite chapter and verse regarding all the phenomenon of the so-called paranormal, but it would no more persuade the unbeliever than it would dissuade the believer. This is a world where each person must judge for self, on what is coming from his conscience, through his conscience.

# THIRTY-FIVE

## THE "SHADES" OF LIFE

The movement of life is not only the greatest mystery, it is the greatest phenomenon. It is the energy eternal. How does it arrive to permeate our bodies, to give them life? Where is its home within these bodies? Where does it go when it leaves these bodies? Does anyone have the answer?

Man has been wondering for many millennia, he isn't any closer to knowing today than he ever was. So to make himself feel better, he has filed his unknowing under the title "Paranormal."

Man may have gained knowledge, he may have gained intellect, in some instances he may feel he has acquired insight, but man has not been illumined.

In trying to step across the ever flowing river from the known to the unknown, he remains teetering on a rock in the middle. He can't go back and he can't move forward. He can only watch the movement of the river called life.

Every man has experienced his own energy. It is the energy that moves his life today.

Many have even experienced the energy that moved life before Adam. This is the energy that flowed within all our ancestors, It is the same energy that flowed before Adam, and it is the same energy that flows today, will flow tomorrow.

The movement of life, the cycle of life, the energy of life, never going, never coming, always being. And yet man prefers not to believe in something as normal as that, He'd rather move it into limbo by referring to it as abnormal. He cannot offer proof to the belief, either way, so he offers theories, conjectures.

Man denies the existence of another dimension, even other dimensions, but he is fascinated by all that is implied.

Ghosts, nah . . . He doesn't believe in them, but tell him more. Around the campfire, around the fireplace, around the table, the stories are told and retold. He knows there is something out there, but isn't sure what that something is. He refuses to make the connection that both he, and what he calls ghosts, are part of the movement of the energy of life. Man himself is a ghost enrobed in matter.

Man, today, prides himself on his intellect, he considers himself most knowledgeable, but man is not attending the university of life, he had barely entered kindergarten. Man, and his ego, refuse to acknowledge that he does not know all and has a long way to go.

It is extremely interesting to read the philosophy of modern man. It is quite informative to wade through his conjectures, his theories, his analyses, of what life is, what death is, what the paranormal is, what normal is. All this baggage loaded into a baggage car, and sent down the rails with never a chance of the rails ever coming together.

Man has created his own myths, his own fairy tales, and is loathe to let go lest they be replaced by a truth he is not ready to face.

Man has a storehouse of memories, they go back in time and they go back to before time. Universal mind is a storehouse of memorabilia. With such mingling and co-mingling is it any wonder that we have the phenomenon of synchronicity? With all minds being one mind, are there really any original thoughts, original ideas? When man indulges himself in what he thinks is original thought, is it? Or is it a powerful system of recall?

Again questions, but where are the answers?

Yesterday the "I" that was . . .

Today the "I" that is . . .

Tomorrow the "I" that will be . . .

What does it mean? It means the "I" never goes anywhere because it is always here in some shape or form.

A "shade" for all seasons, a "shade" for all reasons!

# THIRTY-SIX

## PUZZLED BY "LIFE"

L ife moves, energy propels it, but how far does 'Life" go? Everyone has heard about reincarnation, they have heard about multiple personalities, and they either believe or reject these concepts. Why? Because, either through what they were taught through their religions, or what science has led them to believe, they cannot reach back and give a definite form to the concept.

Man still has a hard time believing in the cycle of life.

Man sees himself as "self," a self in existence for today only. What he either does not want to know, or finds hard to digest, is that there is more to the "I" he sees in his mirror. If he applied the "Alice in Wonderland" concept and looked beyond the "I" in the mirror, he'd see all the other "I's" he ever was, stretching far back in the mirror. No end to the line.

Man is self, he is spirit, individual man consists of the "I" of today and the spirit that is eternal. Life today and life forever.

If man adapts his thinking to this concept, he'll realize that reincarnation, multiple personalities, are as part of his essence as eternality is.

Some would say that because of free will, because of choice, because of the times, because of whatever . . . that multiple personalities cannot exist in one today. Upfront . . . This is their viewpoint, their perspective, their thought, and it does not hang on a valid truth.

Applying the logic of "Mr. Spock," would certainly help to disprove their thinking.

Since the spirit of man is eternal, and it is the spirit that travels the cycles of life, it stands to reason that the self, the "I" of each cycle is a new personality. A new personality enrobed in new matter, but the same spirit. It is spirit who comes and goes. It is spirit that stores the experiences. It is the spirit that retains them as lessons. And it is the spirit that is the storehouse of all the "I's" that have gone before.

Man, as part of a new cycle, develops a personality, lives as that personality, refers to it as the self, the I, and when the cycle is over, man stays, spirit moves on. Spirit retains all the "I's" that attach to it. Spirit has grown itself. Spirit consists of multiple personalities, more than any human can compute.

In the normal course of spirits entry into the human world, the many personalities are kept under lock and key, so to speak, but every so often, they break away from their containment and show up within the structure of the "I" of today. The "I" of today is not equipped to handle more than its own personality and becomes confused when the past personalities of his spirit try to again live a life through him. i.e. Multiple personality disorder. Pandora's box opened. The ghosts of all the personalities of self, of spirit, running amok.

The energy they were, they still are. The energy never left, it was contained within spirit, but a glitch has occurred in the machinery. Man cannot seem to fix it, man doesn't wish to recognize it, because man is not privy to the knowledge behind it.

Reincarnation is more or less a similar theory. An "I" of yesterday has made a choice to return with its spirit and relive the new life spirit has embarked on. For what reason? Man is not privy to this knowledge either. It could be the previous experience was not fulfilled, the lesson not learned, the grade to be repeated. However, the reincarnated "I" comes as a single personality, and not as part of multiple group.

Some have referred to reincarnation as the body being occupied by dead souls. They have completely overlooked the meaning of "Soul." The soul is not a dead anything, it is as alive as when God first gave it life. It is the human matter that dies, not the soul that gave the matter its existence. The soul merely moves on and it has the option, the choice, of a return trip.

Modern man, and we can also include the philosophers from the past, speaks of ego, speaks of mind, but that's all he can do, because he hasn't a clue as to the why, when, who, where, they really are. Man is attempting to use mind, to describe mind, to satisfy his ego. A losing proposition. Man will always remain shackled by his inability to give form, to explain, the unseen part of himself. He dares to explain God, dares to explain the thoughts of God, but he truly does not know God or His actions.

Man would describe the energy that is the movement of all life, but man does not know from whence it comes or where it goes. A true puzzle.

# THIRTY-SEVEN

## PARTING THE CURTAIN

The movement of life is represented by the spirit. Man has always been fascinated by the unknown, the world of spirit. Is there a racial memory at work here that teases but doesn't quite come to fruition in the world of matter?

Man has tried to define spirit, he has tried to give it form, he has tried to communicate with it. He has even given his interest a name, he refers to it as spiritualism. Some have defined spiritualism as a religion, but it is merely a belief.

Ghosts, spirit guides, ectoplasm, etc., man seeks to make contact, to communicate, with whatever is out there. He even goes so far as to allow himself to be conned, he wishes so badly to see into the next dimension.

And yet in and among the hoaxes, something makes its presence known. Someone who was once enrobed in human matter, who has completed a cycle, wishes to communicate that death is just a word. That life goes on, that spirit survives, spirit lives, and this contacter is "living" proof.

It is not so much that man feels a need to know, after all he has been around for a time, has survived without this knowledge. Man simply wants to know, he is curious, he feels something is being kept from him, so he forges on, trying to learn about this other facet of life. The one beyond the physical.

The phenomenon of the spirit world, of the guides, of the voices, is not only of the today. Someone has always managed to reach man through those swirling mists. The son of Abel conversed with an entity he said was God. Many of the well-known names in the Holy books carried on a conversation with someone not seen. The many Gods of the various peoples on this planet have managed to break the barrier and communicate.

No matter how the scientific world, the religious world, the secular world, try to explain what is happening, they are merely shooting clay pigeons in the dark.

The search for edification has gone on for millennias, it will continue. Man is not ready to handle this kind of illumination.

Yes, it is a phenomenon . . .

It will continue to be a phenomenon . . .

It is a valid phenomenon . . .

The truth behind it will remain behind those curtains of mist.

# THIRTY-EIGHT

## *WE ALL SHARE LIFE*

The movement of life belongs to all humans, it is not given to only the learned, all participate in it. The only difference being is the learned and the unlearned approach their theories, their conjectures, from a lesser or greater input from the world of study.

One may have a basic gut reaction, another may find himself arriving at his thought as handed down through the many layers of academia. Both as far apart in their viewpoints as it is possible to be, and neither coming to a definitive conclusion because in the world of man it simply is not there.

Man searches for facts to give credence to himself, his world, his thoughts. He looks to rationalize through science what is all around him. Man has failed to apply his analytical process, he has failed to dissect, he has failed in his understanding, he has failed in all his applications, to consider one thing.

He will never arrive at a definitive conclusion, he will never see beyond all the veils, unless and until, the One who gave him the movement of life, the Creator of all energy, decides to remove, to move aside, those tantalizing curtains.

Nothing is abnormal, nothing is paranormal, all is normal, all is as it should be, all is the movement of life. In time, out of time.

The movement of life takes place on all levels, on no levels.

The movement of life takes place in the past, in the now, in the future.

The movement of life is happening in this moment of life.

The movement of life is not at the center, it is the all.

The movement of life encompasses all that there is.

All the words in existence are the creation of man.

All the theories, the conjectures, are the thinking of man.

All humankind on this planet is a finite construct.

When all humankind is no more, there still will be the world of spirit.

When all humankind is no more, what will happen to all the theories, the conjectures? They will disappear with man.

When all humankind is no more, when there isn't any time, the spirits that live today will go on living, the movement of life will continue.

The river will flow on.

# THIRTY-NINE

## THE QUESTIONABLE CENTER

We move through life, we move through this life, we move through this world, and we expect this world to fulfill us. We are living under a misapprehension. It is not up to the world, it is not up to life, to fulfill our expectations, to fulfill us, this is our job, our responsibility. It is up to us to inspire ourselves, and it is our choice on how we wish to fulfill ourselves.

We have come as spirit, we have clothed spirit with matter, and now we expect that matter to fulfill us in every way. Our perception of why we are here couldn't be more skewed. It is not because of the matter, it is because of the spirit that the journey has been undertaken. As has been said thousands of times before, the choice was made by spirit, the choice was made for spirit, the movement of life was moved to a new locale and spirit was ready to experience that life movement as a human.

It seems that as soon as spirit emerges from the womb clad in matter, it suffers a memory loss. It forgets the reason for the trip and for the rest of its life within that human it seeks the answer to, "Why am I here?"

With racial memory gone, with the answer to "Why?" just beyond reach, spirit must now wait for human matter to make its way through this temporary human life.

Human matter as its own role to play. Through matter man experiences life's movements, but also, through human matter, man affects the movement and he effects the result. Man's struggle has begun.

He goes through childhood, he moves through the various stages of the life of the "I" he is today. He tries to please the human he is and forgets to grow the spirit he also is. Human desires in conflict with the goal of the spirit.

Man is constantly looking for his center, he has forgotten there isn't any center. To have a center denotes there are also parameters, this type of thinking limits the spirit because the spirit cannot have a center. It is itself part of the One who gives it the movement of life and the One encompasses all. It is the eternal and all that is seen and unseen is part of it. No center, no rims, no edges, because if any of these were present they would signify a beginning and an end.

Eternality has no beginning and it has no end.

Eternality has no center, it is all.

# FORTY

## *SEARCHING FOR "LIFE"*

The movement of life, its time, the span between the moment of birth and the moment of death.

However short the time is or however long, this is the movement of life on earth for man. Is this all there is? Some would have us believe so, but "life" goes on.

There is an eternality to life and anyone who doubts need only look around, look at self. Nothing "dies," it recycles itself. Nature, man, and the universe.

Nothing seems to have been written, or addressed, about the possibility that planets also are a part of the recycling process. Using earth time man cannot envision the billions of years that must pass in order for this to take place. But is this beyond the realm of thought? A planet born, a planet filled with life, a planet dying, and after an incredible amount of years, being reborn. Man, as scientist, hasn't advanced the theory, he first seeks evidence. Evidence akin to a needle in a haystack.

The scientific world must move the parameters of its collective mind and it must also move beyond what it thinks is the only evidence . . . human life. Life is all encompassing and life does not limit itself to what we call human. Pushing the parameters back will help expand the limited thinking now in place.

The reference to the needle in the haystack usually indicates the impossibility of finding something and yet there is a fallacy in such thinking. If one moves the parameters back, refuses to limit the direction of mind, does away with false edges, the answer to the problem is simple, can't find the needle in that haystack. . . ? Burn it down, and there is the needle, lying in the ashes.

The definition of life, as seen by man, is restrictive, it does not allow for the movement of "life." It confines thought, it confines life, it wraps it up in the physical. It dams up the movement and refuses to consider the meaning of movement. Life is an ongoing movement, but no one has ever been able to locate this movement. It is in everything and it cannot be touched. It is a current, it is a movement, it is energy, but where is it? It is vital to the life of man, but it transcends man.

No one can escape life. It is with one forever. It comes, it goes, it hasn't any parameters. It encompasses all, it is part of the All, it is All.

Life is in this world, it is in all the universes, but it is not of them.

Life stands alone.

# FORTY-ONE

## *"I"*

The movement of life gives life to the human body. Without this movement our bodies would be absolutely useless. And yet what is the one thing we take for granted? Why the body!

The human puts great store in what he calls the "I" and yet even the "I" is not a part of the body. It is movement within, but its true locale is not known.

The body is a mystery, but it is a mystery of parts, and one by one the parts can be deciphered. But beyond the parts it is a phenomena. It is a container, it holds all that makes the world, the universe go around.

It is a house with many doors and the human who calls it his body is completely unaware of all that goes on behind those doors.

No one can tell the resident of this house how to open the doors. This is the job of the "I" that lives today.

# FORTY-TWO

## *CHOICE*

Spirit was plucked from the world of spirit, injected with the movement of human life, and sent to use it in its new home.

Spirit lives in this home as man, but what man fails to realize is that the spirit contained within does not really look at this world as home.

Man relates to all that is physical, he becomes attached to it. This is his, that is his, all is his, he will fight to his last breath to defend what he considers his.

Spirit looks out through the eyes of man and reflects on the follies of man. It knows this is not its true home. It does not claim ownership, it is merely passing through.

Spirit knows why it is here, man hasn't a clue. So man tugs one way, spirit the other, they are in conflict.

Until man allows spirit to completely take over and show him why he was created man, the conflict will continue. Man was not created man in order to pursue the pleasures of this world. Man was created for the use of spirit. Spirit wanted to experience the movement of life, through man, what it could not accomplish in its real home.

Spirit has found the journey extremely hard. It has experienced, it has learned everything through the auspices of man. Man has used his will power, his choice, his ego, and spirit hung on throughout the bumpy trip. Spirit knows if it doesn't succeed in making man realize the purpose of the trek it will have to be repeated. The human truly gets in the way of God-realization.

Spirit may be realizing that the world of man is filled with pain with grief. That it is a word of darkness, delusion, doubt. It sets about prodding man, nudging his conscienceness, trying to make him realize that unless he mends his ways he will continue the cycle of birth and death. But the mind of man continues to dominate.

Man is wrapped in sowing, he forgets that he will in the end reap what he has sown. He will bear the consequences of his actions. Man is devoted, but his devotion lies in the wrong direction and to the wrong things.

The world of man is not permanent and all the objects are perishable. Man continues to delude himself. He lets his mind run rampant, out of control. Mind serves him well, it follows his dictates. If man made better use of it, the doors he could open would be truly wonderful.

There are many powers within the body called human. They lie dormant, waiting until man decides to access them through the awareness of self.

When man embarks on the inward path he begins to stir up these powers. He begins to see the doors opening. He begins to realize that the movement of life is an inward journey. It flows through soul, it flows through spirit. True life, eternal life, is not a surface life.

Man's choice . . . listen to ego or listen to spirit.

# FORTY-THREE

## *THE ILLUSIONARY DEFINEMENT*

Man has been trying to define the existence of the human for his entire life.

He seeks to define the movement of life. He seeks to define it in relation to the cosmos. Man believes himself capable of such a definition, completely ignoring the fact that it is not possible to do so. He did not create life, he did not create the cosmos, he is part of the plan, he did not create the plan. But man is stubborn, he continues to write the words, diagram the words, draw the pictures, choosing to overlook the fact that never will he arrive at a conclusion. He may seek to open the gates, but he does not have the key. Even the mind he uses to funnel his intellect through does not belong to him.

Every religion has tried to explain, to inform its followers, via a myriad of ways, that each one has the answer, that each one knows, how all came about. The details are mind boggling, the allocation of names to their mythical creations are just as boggling. Not one seems to address a basic fact, it is not in their province. The Force gave man the use of mind, it is a highly prolific mind, it is part of the movement of life, but the Force never gave man the key. So since man does not have the key, he has taken mind and attempted to create his own key. Man has had to wear high-water waders ever since.

Man is a day-dreamer, he creates his legends, he creates his myths and he calls them truths. Man has ascribed much to himself, he has practically deified himself as he seeks to explain who he really is. But man, as a human, who has written the many words to describe himself and now believes he knows all about who he is, has opted to take this ability to describe who God is, and what His plans are, etc., etc., he has tried to step into God's shoes, so to speak. Man, in trying to robe himself in the mantle God wears, forgets his own human self. The man who dares to explain God has yet to create a planet, a sun, a moon, a universe, etc.

He can create the equations, the charts, the graphs, he cannot create original life.

If man proposes, if man supposes, then man also must dispose, because all is illusion, delusion, as seen through the eyes of man.

# FORTY-FOUR

## *CREATIVITY IN ACTION*

God created man, He instilled the movement of life into him. God created woman, the movement flowed from man to woman. But God did not create the eternal conflict between man and woman. This was a creation of the human.

There had to be a gender for the procreation of the movement of life in the human. However, in the eyes of God, all spirits are without gender, all are souls, like the flow of life itself there isn't any demarcation point once the river joins the ocean.

Yet, even when man seeks spiritual ilumination, he seeks to define it according to gender. Man, the human, who has never seen God, has remade Him. One side male, the other side female. Man has genderized God. God, the Holy Spirit without form, has been given a human form.

God created Adam, God created Eve, each to a specific purpose that neither one or the other could manage separately . . . procreation, multiplication. Beyond the one reason and one request, God did not lay down any rules. So how did the role of the sexes come to be? When did it start?

Were the created roles meant to be interchangeable? Hardly, each one was assigned what it was meant to do. It was the human who changed the rules of the game. The human made up the roles that man and woman were meant to play and created the stratification. As civilization, as society, as culture, took place, the stratification calcified.

Men, thereafter, tried to keep women in the roles they had assigned.

Women, tried to move beyond the roles.

Both forgetting that neither could become the other.

Somewhere along the line even God was defined as both male and female, everyone was getting into the divinity act. Myth, created by man, has become so outlandish in its assigning, re-assigning, creating roles for men and women, as visualized by humans, that everyone is confused.

It is a human creativity thing.

It is a human life thing.

It is not a spirit thing.

# FORTY-FIVE

## *IN SEARCH OF SELF*

As humans we move through life doing what needs to be done on a daily basis. Some humans limit themselves as individuals simply because they believe they don't have other choices.

Man, the human, looks at himself and many times cannot even visualize what lies beyond the vision he sees, and the vision he could see if he allowed himself to let go.

Moving through life, as simply a human, ignores the fact that there is also a spirit moving along at the same time. A spirit that is experiencing the today of the human, and also a spirit that enjoyed the yesterdays, as well as a spirit that will enjoy the tomorrows. Now when man takes the time to look into the other world that spirit also occupies, man can see that there isn't any end. Spirit rides the waves of its eternality.

Yes, the Kingdom of God is within. Yes, the movement of life flows through one, but lest the human forget, when it is said the Kingdom lies within, it s not within the human body. The body holds only what the human needs for the today, it is temporary. The Kingdom within is the soul, the spirit, the conscience. This is where the movement of life is.

When one is told that one is the force that makes all things happen, one must pause a moment and analyze that remark. The force, the movement, is separate from the human body. It is a "within" that does not need the human body. It is a "within" that can't be seen, touched, or felt. It is a being within a being and it is complete within itself.

Some speak of a higher self, a lower self, but it is the same self. It is not divided into parts, even though it is a self of many parts. This may seem a convoluted thing to say, but all that comprises the "I" of the human today, and all that comprised all the "I's" that ever were, is enrobed in the self of spirit. Need an example? Look at an orange, look at a grapefruit. Yes even look at a pomegranate. Segments within a whole, seeds within a whole.

When one seeks to embrace what some call the higher self one is merely embracing the spirit that embodies all the "I's." The spirit depends on each I to gain the experience, to learn the lesson that it needs to enable it to rejoin the One and Only Light.

The spiritual mind is a traveling mind, it is as one with the movement of life. One should not depend on ones heart to contribute anything more than its pulsation to keep the body moving through this life. The heart is merely comprised of the same physical matter the body is. It does not transcend, it does not feel, it hasn't any senses.

When the human seeks insight, when he seeks illumination, he does not get in touch with his heart, he gets in touch with his spirit.

If the human would learn to trust his spirit instead of following his ego, he would find his life moving with the knowledge that he may not always be here as a human, but he will always be here as a spirit.

One spirit, one soul, given by God to each and everyone of us for all eternity.

Life does not create the obstacles the human finds flowing through his existence, it is the human who erects all the barriers. He creates the dam so the river is impeded as it flows, as life, toward the ocean.

When man removes the barriers and restores the natural flow, the movement of life, through his life, will generate its own rewards.

Man will have found the self of spirit.

# FORTY-SIX

## *REALITY . . . A POINT OF VIEW*

We call the life we live today, reality, that is our perspective. Is it reality? Or is it simply something we have created as we move through it?

We all have the ability to live life as we wish it to be. Things just don't happen, we initiate them, knowingly or unknowingly, we create the play and we become the actors within that play. Is it than reality? Everything in the life we live today exists as a possibility. As we place our expectations, our beliefs, our hopes, in something, we form the structure. We are the architects of what we call reality. The present, the future, is ours to form. The past is the platform.

We look back, see ourselves on the platform and make a conscious or unconscious decision to follow the self we see standing there. Now if what we see there was good, we can see it reflected in what life is like today. If the experience was not so good, and we brought it forward to today, we have the opportunity to change the movement as of today.

Each and everyone of us has the tools to create new identities for ourselves. What we must keep in mind is that we are not creating a reality, we are creating new roles, just like any actor does. We can flow along with the movement of life wherever it takes us, or we can divert the flow in the direction we wish to go. We are the source.

We create the belief, the belief comes from within. When it surfaces into our outside lives, we think of it as reality. And once out in the outer world we go with whatever belief it is. If it is good, that's fine, if it is bad we still stay with it. We have forgotten that we formed the belief, created the structure and we can recreate, uncreate, do whatever it takes to divert the movement.

Today we allow ourselves to be influenced by the rest of society, we go with its flow instead of creating our own flow. We have tapped into the beliefs of others. We have adopted the values of someone else. We believe what they think matters. We have embraced a perceived reality.

Reality is merely a point of view. The movement of life could be viewed as a reality, and yet all it is is a means of transportation to the true reality. The reality of the life that is eternal, the one beyond the creative structures of today.

Man is a temporary edifice. What he has surrounded himself with is as ephemeral as he is. This is the one reality man refuses to accept, so he goes on impeding the movement of life by obstructing its path with creations without any meaning.

It is not wrong to create the play, to act in the play, as long as man keeps in mind it is only a play.

It is not reality.

# FORTY-SEVEN

## *A FOOT IN THE DOOR*

The movement of life requires an open mind. If the mind refuses to accept its reality, than everything else is without meaning.

So it goes without saying that if one puts all one's beliefs in the world of science, its methods, its conclusions, one has closed one's mind to the reality of the movement of life. All of life is in this movement.

Man has a tendency to chastise life. He blames it for all the misery, the suffering, in the world today. The movement, as life, flows on, it has nothing to do with what is happening in the world today or at any other time. These are merely the scenarios created by the minds of individuals.

It is also true of the scenarios as envisioned by the world of science. It views this world, this universe, humanity, through its microscope. It creates its own "reality," a reality as seen by its collective mind, a reality of a closed mind.

Science doesn't give any credence to the flow known as the movement of life. A flow always in motion, forever in motion. A continuum that the microscope, the closed mind of the scientific world refuses to acknowledge.

Science is not the teacher to the world of the human. The teacher is the spirit. Science, the human, each gaining insight from the force that controls the movement of life.

We are led, we are guided, and all we need is an open mind. We grow, we flow, we manifest. The refuge we seek is at our jumping off place as the movement of life flows on.

# FORTY-EIGHT

## *MANY LEVELS*

The movement of life encompasses all the universes, and all that is harbored in what we call space.

The man called human is an innocent. He attempts to deal with all that is out there within his creation of time. What is time? Time is relative, it does not reach into the domains of existence that man refuses to acknowledge. It does bring, into the existence of man today, what occurred before man's time. It does not readily reveal all the other dimensions, but never-the-less these dimensions exist.

The movement of life, its energy circles through out all that is seen, and unseen. Every thing is connected.

The movement of life empowers us, but we must be willing to accept its power. Once man accepts the power, steps onto the path that hasn't any detours, he will gain unexpected results. He will have taken the key of power and be ready to open all the doors to his well-being, to his spiritual growth. Beyond the open door is the unlimited horizon.

The movement of life encourages the journey.

# FORTY-NINE

## THE SEARCH CONTINUES

Is the horizon always in front of us? Hardly, the horizon surrounds us. It is not just the east or the west, the north or the south. If we stop to analyze it we will understand the limitations we have placed on ourselves.

The movement of life may be a forward movement, but forward happens to be any direction one is facing. So "forward" surrounds us. It is the same when we speak of the past. It does not, cannot, mean a specific direction, because like the movement of life in the "forward" direction, the same move also took place in the "past." The "past" surrounds us, it is in the back, but the back is any direction.

The movement of life surrounds us. It is the circle that does not begin, does not end. It is ongoing. Forward or past, all blend in together.

We do humanity, the human, a great disservice when we try to explain the mystery of his spiritual self. Then stand within the circle and attempt to place it a few thousand years ago, give it a beginning date, so to speak.

The circle of life, the circle of self, does not, by inference, acknowledge such parameters.

Even when man tries to define the Divine and man's ecstatic worship as simply love, nothing more, nothing less, he has missed the point. Yes, there is love, but with love, there is more, and no man can ever explain, define, erect parameters around the Giver, the Creator, the Architect of the circle.

There are the mystics who see visions and set about to explain, give meaning to them.

There are the religions that are ready to educate man about what they say has been revealed.

There are the many humans who create the books filled with their own wisdomic impressions. (This writer does not absolve self!)

But although many may have seen, their eyes have only been shown what is of use to them at this point of their evolvement. The circle keeps turning, the doors, the windows, opening and closing, and the many look out at the quick peek and define it as a great revelation, but dated just a few thousand years into their past. This does not allow spirit full reign, in fact, it reins spirit in.

When one truly desires to see, when one truly wishes to know, one must remove any parameters and look at the horizon with unscaley eyes. The horizon that surrounds one and stretches in all directions, back into a no-time, forward into a no-time, and holding forth in the present time. This is truly "seeing." This is the true faith, born of the soul, of the self, of the spirit, as it emerged from the eternal Light of the Divine. It was not given a limited vision, it was given an all-encompassing one. It is man who is forever looking for a faith he believes he's lost when it is only the belief, as seen through man's construct, that has altered his vision.

Man can search all he wants, but until he makes the conscious decision to accept the fact that; all he ever needs, all he ever wants to know, all he ever was, is, will be, lies within him, not within his body, but within his soul, his spirit . . . he will, perforce, continue his never-ending search.

Belief can be swayed.

Faith is solidly embedded.

# FIFTY

## *GOING IT ALONE*

As the movement of life continues its flow, man within that flow continues to slosh around. He has yet to learn the one lesson.

Why does man find it so hard to understand, that the journey he embarked on so willingly, is a singular trip? It is his soul, his spirit, that is to experience, to learn, in order that it can emerge as pure light when it again becomes one with the Light.

All the gurus in the east, all the mendicants in the west, no man anywhere, can help another transcend. The sage, the seer, the wise man, has not been born, that can perform this miracle. The Tower of Babel came to be for a reason, to house those who babble. Mankind babbles, in whatever language is available, Mankind allows ego to hold sway while it seeks to inform all within range that there is only one way, their way. But this is the fallacy, it is not their way, it is the way of one's own soul, one's own spirit. One need not chant a mantra, one need not pray the words some human has written, one need only to think of one's own soul, one's own spirit and the faith that is a part of it.

The movement of life contains the breath of life, but it is only because the breath is needed for life while it is in time.

We are told to meditate on the breath, it is the gateway, but it is not the breath that is the gateway, it is the soul, the spirit. The soul, the spirit are the cycle, it is not the breath. The movement of life is eternal, it goes on whether one breathes or not.

We all see visions, they are part of the movement of life. We may acknowledge them, we may ignore them, but they are there. We also create our visions, we give form to what the soul, the spirit send forth.

The seed that is so tiny, the diamond that is so brilliant, both encompassed by the soul, the spirit. We are all touched by the Divine, but too many fail to see, to realize, the phenomena. So they continue to spend their earthly time running around looking, asking, for some human to guide them, to lead them. To where? They are there already! Insight, illumination, enlightenment, all part of original faith.

We are the fire, we are the light!

# FIFTY-ONE

## *MAN DID NOT INVENT "LIFE"*

The movement of life did not arrive with first man, the "first" human. Eternality was also not a given for the human.

Man, today, is a mass of contradictions as he sets out to explain his birth, to explain eternal life. He explains one and subsequently negates the other. Man may feel qualified to explain himself, but he cannot explain, positively, the eternal movement of life.

We have been told that the human came into being with Adam, this was the beginning of "life." Anyone that takes the time to think this out would immediately ask the question, "What happened to the eternality concept?" Life is eternal, no beginning, no end. Life already was in the spirit world before Adam arrived on the scene. The human, as we know the term, arrived, but not life.

Man, when he thinks back to Adam, the earth human of his time, must move his mind farther back into the dim recesses of a "before." The spirit world already was, life within its confines stretching in every direction.

The human may also have had beginnings on other planets, in other universes. Why is the assumption made that it was on the planet earth that man first made his appearance?

The human has an alpha and an omega, the spirit does not. When man speaks of Adam as an event that was the beginning of life, he must clarify his words. If Adam is looked at as the beginning of life than life cannot be said to be eternal.

The movement of life is as the wind, it cannot be contained. Within each human lies a propellant, it carries him along through his mortal life, but it also lives as spirit. Within this cycle the human is born, lives, dies. And yet there is something else happening within the cycle, it is an eternality in and of itself. To create a visual, one can take the birth of any child, today. The child is a miracle, in many ways, within that little body is the movement of life, but should the word be "lives?" The scientific world has not managed to find and pinpoint where in the human body are carried the cells of all the lives that contributed to the new life, the baby born today. The amalgam of all that has gone before.

If one should take the span of several generations and put together some pertinent facts about just one individual, one would be awestruck. To take it all back to the birth of the first human and then try to compute how many humans contributed to the makeup of that one baby alive today would be a daunting task.

The scientists make reference to genes. How many genes does each human body have? What is the size of each gene? And does each gene carry all the hereditary genes or only those of one ancestor?

A baby comes endowed with all the genes from the past, on its mother's side, on its father's side. It would be impossible to come up with a figure, even as a start point. Now when we take into consideration its spirit, its soul, and the eternality of them, we would be hard put to add up the numbers.

When the individual of the self looks in the mirror today and believes he is looking at the "I" that he thinks he is, he better think again. The words, "We are more than we think we are," make a lot of sense.

Yes the words, "The movement of life" themselves take on a whole new meaning.

The ocean and the many drops of water that comprise it, has nothing over the human and what comprises him.

The petrie dish in the lab wiggles with life, the scientist say they have discovered life, they can clone individuals, animals, whatever . . .

What is it they are overlooking? Why the fact that they began their experiment using something that already had life, they did not create "life."

# FIFTY-TWO

## "THAT" QUESTION

The movement of life is the key, it holds the answer for the human who seeks to be enlightened. The human who asks, "Who am I?"

The "I" the human is today is what he makes of himself, but the makeup of his physical "I" is who he is.

If the seeker today seems confused it can be understood why, he certainly has a lot on his plate; and should those that today refuse to accept responsibility for their choices, their actions, decide that they have something, someone else to blame, the fallout should be interesting, if not sad. Going back 4.6 billion years to bring the ancestor count of each individual up to speed boggles the mind.

Asking the question, "Who am I?" as one seeks the path of insight, is to beg another, "Who am I not?"

What if today's society, world wide, was informed of any study undertaken to discover just how truly intermingled it is, would it lead to peace? Are there enough lucid minds out there to heed the ramifications of such a study? Would "We are one big family" make sense? Probably not. It is the family that fights, it is the family that wars, it is the family that kills, and it all began with the first family. Cain slew Abel and set the parameters for familial discord.

Man has never risen above it. He may say he seeks insight, enlightenment, a higher road, but it only takes one word, one look, to set him up to fight.

What must man do to overcome this urge? Is it part of his human destiny? Is it part of the human experience, human lesson? Man has populated this planet since it, and he, came into being, that is a very long time to take in order to learn a lesson.

The movement of life through the cycles of human life have flowed for some billions of years on this planet. Is this planet the Alpha, the Omega, for the human? Are similar experiments taking place elsewhere in the universes? And like children who enter kindergarten and progress through various educational grades, are other planets, other universes going through their own lesson? Each on a different level, each in a different grade? Have any graduated? And if we take this educational process through sixteen or so grades, what grade are the humans on planet earth in now?

Will enlightenment only come when they finally graduate?

Graduation for the human in his educational system comes after a finite number of years of attending his schools. But the human himself is finite. Does the matrix that is in place for him also take into consideration his end? The end of the human experiment? And when is that?

# FIFTY-THREE

## *THE NEXT STEP*

M an cannot stop the movement of "life," he does not
control the flow. Can man hasten his enlightenment,
can he gain insight, can he be illuminated? If he can, how
must he go about it?

Should man turn to the East? Hardly, the East has not
shown it has the answer. The West? Not likely, it is still looking for a direction.

Man has been told, time and again, to look within
himself, it is here the answer lies. But before man begins
his inward search, he must first know what it is he wishes
to find. If he is looking to fill material needs, he has already taken the wrong path. It is not the human or any
of his material possessions, that transcend into the world
of spirit, into a higher realm. It is his spirit that does the
transcending, it is his spirit that he must learn to communicate with. No human knows, or can tell another
human what the journey will be like, or even how many
steps it will take.

If any human attempts to tell another that his progression will be made in six steps, eight steps, twelve steps, then
the question should be put forth, "Who do you know that
has reached his destination at the end of whatever steps are

said to be required?" And, "Since you recommend these steps and are said to be participating in the progression where are you at the moment?"

No man can tell another man what it will take, what he needs to know, to do, and what the end result will be. Each man is an individual spirit and as such his progressions are based on his needs. As to when he will reach his final destination? Only the Supreme Being has that answer.

And yet the effort must begin . . .

To look for peace of mind is to attribute to mind a need that it does not have. Mind must stay active, be active. Mind is the propellant for any action to take place, to begin. It is peace for the self one needs to search for, peace to allow its spirit to soar on its journey to the Light.

It is good to research all religions, all beliefs, but it is necessary to separate the chaff from the wheat. If a worthwhile kernel is found, take it to heart, feed it to the spirit, it is only a kernel at a time that a bushel is filled.

Man, being as bereft of spiritually as he is, must make a determined effort to fill the need of the spirit. Spirit does not demand, it waits within the self for whatever kernel is sent its way.

Foremost and utmost, man must know, must remember, must take to heart . . . it is a singular journey. It is a journey for self and it is a unique journey, it is a lonely journey, wisdom cannot be taught, it can only be acquired. And all men are wise men when they finally realize this concept.

One can take a plane, a bus, a train, a goatcart, or walk, looking for the sage, the guru, the wise man. If upon reaching whatever the destination was, one realizes the journey takes place within, and the destination is reached via one's own spirit, one has gained insight. Insight that one need not move the physical body anywhere, because what one is searching for will only be found through one's own spirit.

The physical need not make the trip, the spirit will do it. Why climb a mountain when the Light can be reached from within?

Follow not the heart, follow the spirit. The spirit is life eternal. This is a truth.

# FIFTY-FOUR

## *RIP VAN WINKLE*

The movement of life goes on. It will continue to flow, it will not hold your hand. The movement of life is not a physical movement. Life is not physical.

Why does man, when he embarks on the road to find himself, to find enlightenment, look first for someone to hold his hand?

He looks for a human teacher. The human cannot offer him, nor ever give him, what he seeks. The human may even lead him astray. Does any human know all the questions, does any human know all the answers? "Ask and you shall receive" was not an idle quote.

Seeking and asking, of whom? Here is where most humans take a wrong turn. They ignore those other phrases, "Seek ye first the Kingdom of God" and "The Kingdom of God lies within." The teacher is not on the outside, the teacher is on the inside, and the teacher does not require any coin of the realm. Nor must one endure outer hardship to take the journey. The diamond of wisdom is not a product designed by man. It is not a tangible item. It lies within the self created by God. And of course the follow-up, "Whatever you need, you already have."

Taking one phrase or taking them all, the one message that comes across is that within lies everything and within the self is where the journey takes place.

To search for any meaning in this journey called life, in the movement of life, is to ignore the one word, "Life." Life the force like no other. Man can no more avoid life than he can ascribe a meaning to it, he is surrounded by it. Life is the "Light." Life is the "Divine Being." Life is the "Creator." Life is a gift, it is a shared movement.

The world of spirit is a world of eternal life. The life within the human is to experience it in a different fashion. The spirit that wishes to experience it, through the human, makes the choice, makes the decision, and is willing to accept everything that comes its way by action of the human.

So we say that everything that happens to the human is by his own actions, and everything the spirit experiences and learns is by those actions. This is the meaning of life, this is the reality of it. Life in and of itself is "real," but it is not a realness that takes place in the world of the human. If anyone is looking to put "real" into their life they will be sadly disappointed. What devolves to realness are the actions taken, the illusions created, the choices, the decisions, made by the human. He is the one creating the "I" personality he is today. He is the one seeking meaning to his own actions. He is the one ignoring spirit while catering to the ego of the "I." He is the one ignoring his own inborn faith.

Man is short-sighted indeed. He reaches back in his time to find the enlightenment found by a few some 2000-3000 years ago. He elevates to a status on a par with the Creator. He views as unparalleled the wisdom that was attributed to these few. He begins a search for spiritual rebirth. What has he overlooked? He cannot rebirth his spirit, spirit is everlasting. He cannot find enlightenment via the efforts of another. If any of this could be accomplished wouldn't it have taken place already?

The spirit that functions within everyone of us does not need to be awakened. Spirit does not sleep. It is part of the movement of life and it goes where life takes it.

Physical man is the sleeper, it is he that must awaken, that must open the door to the inner self if he wishes to see the "Light."

# FIFTY-FIVE

## *DISCONNECTED*

Man feels a separateness, he feels as if the movement of life has nothing to do with him. He does not feel as one with his spirit, with his planet, with his universe. This is a perfectly legitimate feeling. Man is a separate entity. Physical man is merely an end to a means.

It is the spirit living through man that is of import. It is the spirit that is connected, it is the spirit that moves with life, through life, that flows as one with all that is seen and unseen. Like the river to the ocean, like the drop of water in the ocean, there isn't any separation. All flowing, all living, as one.

As the child, that is born today, is comprised of all that came before, it too is part of the whole, but must do its living as a single entity, so the spirit it is, can experience the world of man anew.

It is the drop within the flow contributing to the whole and yet still one drop.

It is not the physical that survives, it is the spirit that once gave it life that moves on, goes with the flow, becomes One once again.

# FIFTY-SIX

## *MOVING CLOSER*

Believe in the spirit of the self, it is the internal light that moves one ever closer to the eternal light. The movement of life, the movement of light, and spirit a part of both.

And if one is a seeker and if one is looking for truth, one must come face to face, as it were, with the fact that . . . In the world of spirit there isn't any gender. In the world of spirit there isn't any religion. In the world of spirit there aren't any politics. In the world of spirit there aren't any humans. The way of enlightenment is for all, it is not wrapped up in the trappings of the human. If one wishes to embark on the path, one must first divest one's self of the "human" mentality and of the human ways. This is insight.

Man cannot comprehend all that his outer world consists of, it is impossible for him to understand his inner world or the world of spirit. To go beyond the world of spirit is to attempt to use words that do not exist to cover an unknown that is beyond knowing. Man has a long way to go, his spirit, an even longer one.

As a human, man can seek, he can search. He can listen to all who believe they have something to say, but it is a human search, a one on one with another who is also searching. So who is it doing the teaching and who is it doing the learning?

Both are limited because all stops at the threshold of the human existence. Does the spirit that crosses the threshold retain all that was said? Or does it know already what the human is so desperately in search of?

Can any human be enlightened during this life, in this time? For those who would have us believe this can be done one would ask, "Why then have you not moved on, why then does your spirit keep returning, why is it that it has not been reabsorbed into the Light?"

Enlightenment, illumination, perfection, if all it took was one human lifetime, there would not be the need for a 4.6 billion year, and still counting, struggle.

Man has been following man in his search for spiritual illumination, spiritual fulfillment, this has not brought him any closer to his desire.

It is time to discard this particular path and take the path of one's spirit. Spirit has been on the approach path since it was just a spark.

Is it any closer to its destination, its objective? That answer is known only by the One.

# FIFTY-SEVEN

## *THE CONTAINER*

The movement of life teaches. What does it teach? Everything!

If man seeks the path of enlightenment, he must first begin by admitting that he does not know anything. He must open the eyes of the human he is so he can reach the spirit that occupies the vessel.

Man puts entirely too much store in the vessel itself, while spirit simply walks away when it is time. Spirit knows, man has yet to acknowledge the situation.

All the ceremonies, all the rites, all the words that have become part and parcel of all the religions, have led to a belief that they are important, that they have meaning. They do not. As far as spirit is concerned, as far as the Creator of that spirit is concerned, they merely hold man back, they get in his way. Should they have had any meaning, man would have reached the enlightenment of the self ages ago.

All men walk in sand, they do not leave any footprints behind. The step made in the sand is already disappearing before the next one is placed. There is a meaning to this, it informs man that he, as a human, is not meant to last. A truth man would prefer not to face, so in order to give himself a type of substance, he surrounds himself with material things. There are some that would rather lose their lives than their possessions. Man and his possessions, reality gone awry. He has misplaced the spirit of self. He has given pride of place, not to spirit, but to the material. He has taken action, he has made the choice, he has opened the wrong door, he has stepped onto the wrong path. What happens now? The movement of life, in time will supply a graphic demonstration. Man will soon be posing the question, "Why?"

No the human is not required to spend the life he has been given by sleeping in a ditch, clothing himself in rags, or living hand to mouth. He can supply himself with the necessities, even luxuries, as long as he has his priorities in order.

To search for enlightenment is to be mindful that the movement of human life is from second to second and the movement of life as spirit is for all eternity.

It is never material possessions that are important.

It is never the container that is of any import, it is always its content.

# FIFTY-EIGHT

## *REALIZATION*

As man moves through life, as he seeks to fulfill his destiny, one of the goals he seeks is enlightenment. In its very context this means to give information; to instruct; to make clear; etc. Simply, knowledge gained and received, is this how the seeker interprets it? Or is what is being looked for more esoteric?

To be enlightened by everyday knowledge, or to be enlightened by a truth that transcends such mundane information?

The movement of life encompasses all kind, but not everyone searches for the more profound. Those who have embarked on the path to enlighten the self must differentiate between the profound and the mundane.

When the realization comes to them that life is not easy, that it has, and demands, certain obligations, are they enlightened?

When the realization comes to them that the material things they crave are really not important, have they become enlightened?

When the realization comes to them that they are the creators of their own problems, have they become enlightened?

When the realization comes to them that they can free themselves by making better choices, decisions, have they become enlightened?

Well, yes and no. The light bulb may have lit up above their heads, but in its light they may have merely discovered the mundane rules of the everyday. They aren't any closer to finding spiritual enlightenment than before the bulb began to glow. They have simply recognized the facts of life within the movement of life. The spiritual well has yet to be tapped.

When man seeks to bring up the bucket of spiritual enlightenment from the well, he finds the task is far from easy. This bucket is filled with the profound. It is filled with all that the spirit has learned as it completes a cycle. It is filled with universal wisdom. It is filled with gifts from the Creator. It is one heavy bucket. And as man tugs on the rope he finds that he must give in order to receive.

He must give his faith, he must have faith, in his Creator.

He must walk the path, he must step in the footprints left by his Creator.

He must put his Creator first, above all things, if he wishes to experience true enlightenment, if he wishes to walk in the Light.

He must face the truth, that as man his options are limited, but as spirit they are unlimited.

"Enlightenment" or enlightenment, there is a difference.

# FIFTY-NINE

## *THE FLOW OF SPIRIT*

As one moves forward within the movement of life, one finds that the flow does not stop at the threshold. One finds that what is defined as wisdom on this side, becomes "Illumination" on the other.

Man believes and feels that he is wise once he learns certain facts abut life.

Man feels that he is wise when he applies a common sense rational to his life.

Man feels that he is wise when he demonstrates his knowledge of the ways of the world.

All this does not translate or imply a true "wisdomic" knowledge. It is merely getting along in this world.

To acquire a wisdom that goes beyond the world of to-day, man must seek, through the inner self, his spirit.

It is the spirit that has the ability to show man what wisdom really is.

It is the spirit, that can open the doors to what it has learned in its cyclical travels.

It is the spirit that can see into the new dimension and also look back at other dimensions.

It is the spirit that has made the walk, and continues to make it.

It is the spirit that translates earthly wisdom into spiritual illumination.

Spirit moves, spirit flows, spirit is forever.

# SIXTY

## *A LONG WAY DOWN*

The movement of life goes on, will go on. The human, today, will continue to seek. Enlightenment, illumination in the context as seen by our society today, will continue to flow to the East, and from the East to the West. The human is not ready to give up his individual belief and he is determined to spread that belief. He is not sure why the entire world does not see things his way, whatever his way is. He believes he has arrived, but he hasn't even left the station.

The diverging paths of the many religions must come to the realization that God doesn't care how you are making the trip, just as long as you are. He doesn't recognize any one path anymore than another, and He doesn't recognize the anger that trods those paths.

Do any of those who would practice their way and would deny another his way believe the Creator is willing to accept their prayers over the others? Prayers to Him are through one's spirit and they are meant to be untainted. If the human is busy killing while he prays, and is also asking to be saved at the same time, he has missed something in his belief, his religion. He has misplaced faith. He is qualifying his request, he is making a mockery of his request, he is sending a tainted prayer to his Creator and hoping it will be granted.

Certainly he has not taken the high road. The high road demands that he first examine himself and his intentions. He cannot even begin the climb until he has cleaned his outer house, and set his inner house in order.

Any attempt to climb the high road without the proper preparations will only result in a fall and the fall is a long way down.

# SIXTY-ONE

## *SAY WHAT?*

Spirit lives forever, the human does not, and yet man couples the two as if they were a single entity. Man calls the spirit, a human spirit, but is it? What is human about it? Man does not know what it looks like, what it feels like, and where it is located. Does this stop man from talking about it, writing about it, and trying to make himself sound like an authority on spirit? Hardly! Man is coasting along on an assumption, as well as his own definition of a nomenclature of his own construct. He uses the word spirit and the word spiritual to denote various meanings of choice, he can make them mean whatever he decides they should mean. So when someone decides to write about spirit, about spirituality, they must first qualify which of the definitions is applicable. Man sees what he wishes to see, and even then he is unsure about what he is seeing, because, in truth, there is nothing for him to see.

When man, and his mate, moved out into the world, they quickly became aware of their own transformation as well as their new home. Thus began the concentrated effort to regain what they had lost. Did they think of themselves as spirits? Did they believe they were human spirits? They were entities who were now known as humans. Was a spirit part of this construct?

The questions don't go away, each answer simply leads to a new question. The human asks them, the human answers them, where is spirit in this equation?

Over the course of human existence, man has striven, has strained, has used a variety of methods to open those invisible doors. Has he been successful? Some say they have, they say they have gained insight, have gained enlightenment, have gotten in touch with spirit's true home. They follow the dictates of "Know thyself, go inside of self and all will be revealed." When the method called, "meditation" is used, who is it they get in touch with, who is it that speaks to them? Do we know or are we again assuming?

Surrounded by the spirit? The spirit within the body? The spirit, like thought, coming and going? One spirit, like the trunk of a tree, diverse spirits like the limbs of the tree, each human like a leaf on the tree? Who is to say?

Spirit, faith, belief? We are the universe, the universe is us, we are one, why then if all is one do we have so many off-shoots? A spirit for each of us, a faith of our own, a belief that is not of one religion, but of many. Is all really a one harmonious whole and has man caused his own disharmony? To what purpose? As we all approach that one and only door, do some really believe we are separated as to that belief, that religion, that gender, that race? Does not such a belief fly in the face of the one truth?

The human sets the parameters, the human asks each of us to follow, to believe, a certain leader, a certain group. Where lies truth? The human seems to be all over the place but not in the right place. The spirit, the soul, the conscience, the self, manifested in one human being, and yet such thinking seems in direct opposition to, "We are one." Attunement, cooperation, unification, are the responsibilities required of us as we seek to put in action the theory of oneness, but in all of the human existence, we have never even come remotely close. Are we misunderstanding the message, is the human approach not getting it?

We meander, we stumble, we bumble, we keep missing the truth because it seems to be enmeshed in man's own interpretations. We, as single entities, and we as groups, simply do not know who we are. We cannot agree on what we are made of, where we came from, and we certainly haven't a clue as to our destination.

What man thinks is not what is necessarily so, what man writes is what man thinks and around we go again.

Man is said to have free will, he is said to have choice, and yet it seems he does not have the final say. Where does one begin and the other end? If we are spirit and spirit is "life," is spirit living it or are we living it through mind, through thought. Than again are mind and thought separate parts of spirit? If God, who we are part of, gave us life so He can live it through us, what does this say about the Ultimate Power? Why go through an existence through man when the experience can be manifested with a snap of the "fingers," a mere thought? Man has rationalized everything through his perspective, he had even given fellowman all of God's reasons for doing what He does. To gain such extraordinary insight, man has made himself a co-Creator of his world, his universe, but it seems he has neglected to assume responsibility for his actions.

And lest man forget, he is only man. He will never transcend, he will never move into another realm, he will return to the dust that he is. Can he still rationalize himself into the role of a co-Creator when he stops to think about it?

# SIXTY-TWO

## *HE WHO WATCHES*

Yes, God does hold our hand, as He also holds us in the palm of his hand, that is a given. Having said that, the statement needs to be qualified, it is the human who has given God these human attributes. The human cannot say, with any authority what it is God looks like.

Okay, back to the first sentence, God does watch over us, but what He does not do, and should not be expected to do, is live the life He has given us, for us. We are responsible for our actions, we must be aware that it is up to us to live it according to His precepts. Everything that happens in our lives is not the result of God's will, if it were, free will and choice would be meaningless, would not be a factor. And there would surely be no need for life as a human.

If the human makes a stupid decision because of his free will, because he has the option of choice, he cannot turn around and blame God for the result. Conversely, if he lives his life in a manner that is rewarding, he cannot give God credit, he is simply living life.

God loves all humanity. He does not distinguish or favor anyone. It is man who assigns the various roles, creates the strata, instigates the split. It is man who wraps himself in a coat of various beliefs and in doing so regards himself as special.

He will watch over, but He will not lead our lives for us.

# SIXTY-THREE

## *THE ARROW*

Take worship, take its many forms, take its many paths, take its diversity. Can man attribute all this to God, to God's involvement or should man face the truth squarely and acknowledge that God did not have a hand in this mix. Should man, once and for all, say he did it, he did it his way, using free will and choice to create a home for his beliefs?

If the human would acknowledge this fact it might change his future. Since man arrived on the scene he has made his own life miserable by his choices and he seeks to claim what he has chosen devolves from God. Looking at such thinking with an analytical eye exposes the holes. If such thinking had any validity the human would not keep stepping off the path to seek another path, and when that path leads to a dead-end, to reverse the self and seek a new direction. The problem here lies in the fact that the new direction is not necessarily the right direction, it may be merely a new choice.

Some, who call themselves intellectuals, view our world, our universe, as an absurdity. In their eyes it may appear so, but it is only the human who surrounds himself with an air of sophistication that sees an absurdity and overlooks the part the human plays in making it so.

2521-MARC

The easiest way to dismiss anything one knows nothing about is to call it absurd, using this analogy, the human emerges as the most absurd.

One universal mind or a myriad of individual minds and man has yet to come to a meeting of them. Take anything in the life of the human entity and the human can ascribe whatever he chooses. He can make it a spiritual moment, he can make it a learning moment, he can make it a getting-in-touch-with-the-self moment, he can . . . Well, anything. He is only limited by mind. He is creating a milieu to live his life in. He is using free will, he is choosing, he is living the human life.

We also have man in search of his spirit, in search of spiritual enlightenment, in search of transforming himself. The word spirit and all the derivatives, merely point up the fact that man hasn't a clue.

Following the arrow of choice does not necessarily mean following the right arrow and it does not mean that man even sees the arrow.

Man is notorious for the blinders he wears.

# SIXTY-FOUR

## *WHAT IS LIFE? WHAT IS SPIRIT?*

Everyone speaks glibly about life, about spirit, but are they really aware of the true meaning, the true nature of either?

The dictionary has a definition for life, as well as a definition for spirit, but one must keep in mind who compiled it, who invented the words, who gave them their meaning. It was that strange entity called a human, and, as the human is limited to his perspective, his definitions are not necessarily all encompassing ones. He lacks a certain knowledge. When the human relays information about life, about spirit, it is conjecture, pure and simple. He attributes human characteristics to what is not human, it seems he finds it difficult to relate on any other level, especially the invisible one. So life is personified, spirit is personified, a form is visualized, the human now can relate. He is seeing all through human eyes.

When the human takes the time to really analyze his beliefs he finds his theories are suspect.

Life . . .

Life is everywhere, it surrounds everything, it encompasses all, and yet, has anyone really seen "life?"

The same can be said of spirit. Who can claim that they have seen spirit?

Life and spirit may give the human the means to exist, but they are the ephemeral part of the physical body. The body may be said to be a human person, but not life, not spirit. These go on even when the human is no more, they survive because they are the eternal forces.

Personality, characteristics, are developed by the human as he makes his way around the circle within each cycle. Life, spirit, the invisible energy, the invisible force cannot be said to have either. Can an essence be given a form? Can thought generate the form? Can the essence be given a personality, characteristics?

Man deludes himself. He forms groups and within those groups man forms, and re-forms, his beliefs, his thoughts, his ideas. He seeks to give a validity to these by humanizing, personalizing, what is beyond his understanding.

Is it wrong? No, one cannot say it is "wrong" one can probably say it is a chosen path to make what is a mystery more believable, more understandable. Man has a need to build his idols, his icons. He needs the visual to help him give his beliefs substance.

Life, spirit. God, a force, an essence, an energy, this is the universe. As man has felt the need to visualize the ultimate, it seems the ultimate has had a need to visualize the universe. Man has been allowed to see . . .

What happens now? What is there left to visualize?

# SIXTY-FIVE

## *READ ALL ABOUT IT*

The books, the stories, are to set our minds at rest. They tell us what to expect, what we will find when we cross into the final frontier. The question arises, "What makes them believe they know?"

We cross, and, supposedly, are met by every member of the family that has preceded us, and just about every Tom, Dick, and Harry, we ever knew. Somehow, no matter how authoritatively they write about this event, it is a stretch to believe.

Can all these entities just be hanging around on the other side of "St. Peter's Gate" with nothing to do except wait for us? How boring! How stultifying! Aren't they supposed to be learning new lessons, moving into higher dimensions, even returning once again to work on the self within the parameters of the human?

Is it possible that what is said to be seen is merely a delusional illusion? An illusion brought on in the mind of the viewer because these are the viewer's expectations?

In the crowd on "St. Peter's" side, the viewer sees diversity, the viewer claims to see children, born and unborn. The viewer claims to see peoples of all ages and relatives galore. Others have markedly different opinions about what they see. All on the other side revert to an age around thirty, thirty-five. They aren't old, they aren't young, they've been frozen in a time warp that does not exist.

When such a difference in the optical outlook takes place can it not be said that the viewer has done his own creating? If man creates his reality on this side, why wouldn't his mind create his "reality" on the other side?

Does one automatically gain in wisdom when one steps through those gates? Or can it be said that it also has to do with the age of the soul, the spirit? A "young" soul, not necessarily a young person, that crosses over would certainly not gain great wisdom if it hadn't been around to experience, to learn, the lessons in this dimension.

Than, again, when anyone crosses over, the chain, by necessity, must be broken, the people left behind, must move on, and those who have crossed must move on. They can no longer hover over those left behind to "hold" their hands, so to speak. If this were the case, no one would ever grow their way towards perfection because they would still be vicariously involved with the humans they left behind.

Emotion, pain, etc., part of the human sense package, also a part of the spirit package?

We may all be part of the universe, we may all be part of the universal mind, we may all exist together in the now, but there must be a delineation or we'd all go crazy trying to live on all levels at the same time.

Some gates, some doors, may open, but at the same time others must close.

Each human, each spirit, each soul, has a goal. It is a "personal" goal and to reach its fruition each must work on the self as an individual.

The words the human uses to define himself and his expectations are human words. These words lose all meaning when the human ceases to exist.

Memory accompanies because it is part of the experience, part of the lessons, it is with the spirit, the soul, throughout eternity. It is also the report card.

It is said that we are energy, within the package, without the package. Is energy also love? Love is an emotion, how is it reflected in memory? Memory is energy, like electricity, it has its function. Memory is stored, it is filed. Where and how . . . under the category of memory? Or simply a blip in the energy chain?

We also find the authors of many such books saying they are led, they are guided. Well and good, but is the guide simply there own spirit? Why do they insist on placing the entity in a certain category? These are earth definitions of people, and as such what is of the human does not transcend, as much as their minds delude them into thinking it is so.

On "St. Peter's" side of the gate, are spirits comprised of energy. They do not have any human characteristics, features, or whatever.

As they say, imagination is powerful and one can "see," in one's imagination, whatever one wishes to see.

The spark of light that we were when we separated from the One and Only Light, we still are. Light, electricity, energy.

While in the human, we still are the spark of light, and when we discard the human body, we remain that spark of light. Nothing more, nothing less. Ethnicity, race, gender, all belong to the human and remain with the physical as it returns to dust. The spark continues the journey.

Those who raise expectations of what the human can expect when the crossing takes place, are doing the human a great disservice. The human never makes the crossing. The spirit of light does and no one can tell anyone else what this spirit will encounter. It is the spirit's journey, it is the trip it continues on as it makes its way to rejoin the light.

It is amazing that the One that knows, says nothing, while those who haven't a clue say and write reams.

The stories are good, they sound believable, are they real?

They are real in the minds of those who relay them and those who wish to believe them. They are even true in that respect. They are created reality as seen from this side of "St. Peter's Gate." What "St. Peter" sees and what is actually there will be part of the transcendental experience each of us will undergo, as spirit.

The universe is filled with spirits, as it is filled with stars, each star following its own path, each spirit doing the same.

# SIXTY-SIX

## THE BOOKS OF LIFE

Who really does keep the books of life? Why is it so hard to trace the foot prints of man?

Before the advent of writing, as we know it, before the advent of record keeping, as we know it, someone kept track.

Man has always left a trail. He has kept memory alive, he has recorded the memories of others, he has left evidence that he has been in the stories he has told.

And yet in spite of his best efforts, the winds of time keep obliterating what he leaves behind.

Today's, yesterday's, papers, books, edifices, deteriorate, the stories undergo change as each new storyteller relates what he heard and embellishes it before passing it on. The more time that passes the more is lost. What is man doing to his own heritage? Even when, by accident, he manages to stumble upon some old "foot prints" in his eagerness to preserve them, he actually destroys them.

We can still find, on our planet today, a few who have one foot in the dim past, while living in the today, but even that foot planted in the recesses of time, does not go back far enough in time.

Could it be that such peoples live in a dimension that is not one that modern man lives in? A spiritual one, as well as a physical one? Is their reality a different reality?

In the frenzy of modern man to bring everyone on this planet into his world of modernity, he has managed to destroy many ancient cultures. He has pulled, dragged, shoved, done everything in his power to make those he calls "backward" accept the modern way. In so doing, any lingering footprints have been eradicated or are in the process of being blown away. Yes, modern man, himself, is destroying the heritage he seeks to find, to uncover. Once everything is destroyed in the process of modernization, man can never go back, even to find his shallow roots, let alone his deepest roots.

Today's man cannot step back in time into the reality created by those who lived back then. He cannot step into their dreams. He cannot step into his neighbor's dreams. We can live parallel lives, but we cannot live the same lives.

Modern man, ancient man, also fight over land. Ancient man says modern man took away his land, maybe so, but ancient man doesn't say who he took the land away from, his memory doesn't allow him to travel back in time to that day. The planet didn't come with people, all peoples had a beginning on it. They arrived, from where is not known, but arrive they did and move around they did. The land belonged to no one, the land still does not belong to man. Never, ever, was the human of long ago given a piece of land here or apiece of land there, no man owned the planet therefore no man could give it away. The humans who arrived from wherever were given usage of this planet but they were not given the planet. It is man himself who began to portion it, to establish ownership. He created the laws that apportioned it and he created the wars to fight over it. If all mankind disappeared today, who would the land belong to? It would belong then, as it belongs now, to the

One who put it here in the first place. In all the time mankind has been occupying this planet, this earth, when it is time for him to leave does he take his allotted portion with him? Never!

We are not the owners, we are the lessees, and we occupy all on a temporary basis. We are simply passing through. Knowing this as fact, why is it man still wars over what is not his?

The Books of Life record man's footprints and it seems they also make them disappear. Is there a lesson here for mankind to learn?

# SIXTY-SEVEN

## TRYING TO UNDERSTAND

Who can understand the mind of man?
Who can understand his motives?
Who can understand his desire?
Who can understand his need to preserve his heritage?
Who can understand his wish to build museums to house his treasures?

Who can understand his stupidity when he turns around and destroys, by whatever means, the unreplaceable artifacts that are a clue to what he once was?

Who can understand man?

Much has been made of the Scrolls of the Dead Sea. Ancient man trying to preserve his heritage on copper, on leather, on whatever he could find and hiding it in caves, in vessels, in out of the way places.

The mind not cognitive of the fact that some of the writing materials would not survive normal deterioration, and the mind itself of two minds. One it seems, that no one would locate what had been hidden, and two, that someone would find what had been hidden.

Man is an expert in displaying his naiveté when it comes to preserving his ancestry.

It reminds one of the ant and its industrious ways. It is all over the place, storing, building, etc., only to have someone come along and destroy all its efforts.

The saga of the Scrolls. Someone took the time to write everything down in the archaic language, archaic thought, that never made it into the known. How old are they, when were they written and before they came into existence what was? The estimate is that they were written in two thousand B.C., or thereabouts, and could have been the birth of the Old Testament. They were found sometime around 1947, were regarded as a puzzle, as a bone to squabble over and at this late date, some fifty plus years, nothing has changed. Man continues to muddy his own waters.

Have the Scrolls taught us anything?

They have taught us that man is still limited in what he knows about himself, his ancestry.

They have taught us that man is almost adverse to living the life of peace he claims to want.

They have shown us that in one area of the world some recorded information was found pertaining to that area and its times.

They have taught that, as much as many have hated to admit it, in other parts of the world similar procedures were used to record and hide.

They have taught that it is still man who writes, man who records, and all is still subject to his own interpretations.

They have taught the records found were not a beginning of anything, simply an interim record.

They have taught that before these records, there were others, man has yet to discover them all.

They have taught that it is possible the cache may have been one of many such caches. Without a modern day copier, the writers may have hidden many such copies, hence the seeming duplication in words, in works.

They have taught that man has much to learn and he has yet to find all the answers, let alone solve the puzzles.

They have taught that time is an illusive commodity since time, in and of itself, does not exist.

They have taught that no man will ever understand it all.

And yes, they should also be teaching modern man that as he seeks to move out into space and as he seeks to make contact with . . . whatever entities reside out there, to look back and use the Dead Sea Scrolls as a lesson.

The recordings, the books, the whatever, that are being crammed into capsules and catapulted out into space, will be as difficult if not impossibe for anyone to translate. The senders are making the assumption that whoever stumbles on these items will be able to make heads or tails out of them. The Dead Sea Scrolls, along with just about anything we have unearthed todate, prove the fallacy of such an assumption. A bunch of photos could very well be the answer.

# SIXTY-EIGHT

## *THE SIREN NAMED EGO*

If we, as individuals, could really see past ourselves, what doors would we seek to open? If we ignored the siren call of the outer to focus on the inner would we transform ourselves?

There is much truth in saying the outer is holding us back. The outer, as self, and the outer as humankind. Humankind has evolved, it has devolved, and it is still doing so. However it is doing so within the parameters of its outside image. It has yet to make the same progress within itself. The race of human still cannot see, or wishes not to see, that to make progress as individuals, it must be as individuals within the self.

Man has gained in knowledge even as he refutes some of it. Knowledge is knowledge, it is all encompassing, it is what one does with it that makes the difference. The most significant part of that knowledge is that we do not know it all. We are still in the "K" class in terms of what we know as opposed to what the universal mind knows.

As we move with life on the outside, life is also moving us on the inside.

We, as humans, tend to see ourselves within the parameters of a higher self and a lower self. In such thinking we are demonstrating that we have the knowledge, but we are not using it correctly.

We are spirits, light descended from the One and Only Spirit. It is not a Higher Spirit or a Lower Spirit it is the Only Spirit. We are the sparks of light. We are not higher sparks, we are not lower sparks, we are a created light. As such "we" live in human matter, it is the living that we do in the outer that creates the schism. It does not make for a higher self or a lower self, it makes for a duality within the ego that thinks of itself as the ultimate self.

Since none of this is real as we recognize real, than it must be a creation as envisioned by the ego to give itself status on various levels.

It is the ego that refuses to believe in the oneness in the spark of light.

It is the ego that calls out to its human self.

It is the ego that manipulates that self.

It is the ego that makes such a loud noise that the spirit within cannot make itself heard.

It is up to us, as individuals, to make the choice, listen to the ego or listen to the spirit.

# SIXTY-NINE

## *I CAN'T HEAR YOU*

Something seems to be wrong in our world. We have some countries overrun with people, poorer than poor, and yet there are temples, churches, places of worship, that are beyond count. The construct of these places beyond imagination. More money has been spent on them than it would cost to take care of the entire country. The people are devotion personified, they pray, they give and yet . . . nothing changes. Everything is as it was and the people keep getting poorer, while they spend every cent they have on their places of worship. Obviously no one has taken to heart, or takes to heart, the saying about not amassing earthly treasures.

Is this a complaint? Is this a denigration of worship? No and no. What is being said here is that if the Supreme Being is ignoring what is being petitioned it might be He's telling the people, and their leaders, you must help yourselves. Could be a message is being relayed i.e. " I've given you gifts, it is up to you to use the gifts. Do not ignore them and ask for more. You are in the predicament you are because you would rather keep asking rather than buckling down and doing. I gave you a life to live, I gave you gifts to live this life, and I am disappointed in how you've chosen to live your life and use your gifts.

"Your edifices do not impress me, they will not transcend with you. Taking and using your last penny to build them is foolish. I do not dwell in these marble halls of yours, I dwell in your heart.

"There is nothing wrong with what I have done, there is nothing wrong with what I have decided not to do. It is you, the people who have chosen how you wish to live.

"You call me God, you call me the Supreme Being, those are your words, they are human words. As the Spirit I am, I will always listen, I will always help, but I do not suffer fools gladly. The hands outstretched to me are begging hands, they request, they ask, they demand, they say please give. I look down and say, 'I already gave, what have you done with my gifts?'

"My world is a perfect world and if it seems otherwise in your eyes, it is because you have made it so.

"Do not try to impress me with your temples, your churches, impress me with your approach via the inner spirit.

"I do not choose to hear you, because you do not choose to hear me."

# SEVENTY

## *THE SQUARE PEG . . .*
## *THE ROUND HOLE*

Yes, life is a movement.
Yes, there is the movement of life.

Although man is aware, and although he attempts to define, can he? Can he explain, does he really know, or is it simply ego talk?

Man finds it difficult to accept the fact that there are certain things he will never know. To fill this void, he puts forth his opinions, his perspectives, his definitions. He creates a slant and then manipulates it to fit.

Is man on the right track or is he so far afield that, if and, when the door should ever open he will be more than astounded, he will be shocked?

The movement of life is part of man's experience. Man the human, man the individual, travels the escalator during his cycle within the circle. He has been taught, but has he learned? Infinity in back of him, infinity in front of him, he stands in his moment in time, hugging his experience in the now, because it is only the now that he remembers.

Man . . . the square peg, in the round hole.

# SEVENTY-ONE

## THE MIND . . .
## AN UNKNOWN LABYRINTH

Science, today, would like to believe it has discovered what the mind is, what it does, how it works. Has it? It has not!

What has been uncovered is but a drop in an ocean filled with so many hidden dimensions that it is quite possible man will never uncover all the probabilities, all the possibilities.

The mind, the soul, the spirit, the human, the circle, the cycle, each a mystery in its own right, each a mystery as part of the whole.

Try as the human does to solve such puzzles, it seems he will forever be doomed to conjecture. The curtain of gauze might as well be lined with lead because the penetration it allows is so limited.

Man walks the labyrinth of his life, he lives the labyrinth of his life, he is lost in the labyrinth of the movement of life.

A maze without any exits.

# SEVENTY-TWO

## *MOVING MIND*

Or moving mind to the next level . . .
Science is defined as a systematic knowledge of natural or physical phenomena; ordered arrangements of facts known under classes or heads; etc.

Is science absolute knowledge or is it merely a study of various phenomenon? And when it presents anything as a fact, isn't it simply a perspective?

After all phenomenon is defined as anything appearing or observed, especially if having scientific interest; a remarkable person or thing; sense appearance as opposed to real existence.

Mind moves the scientific world along as it pursues a study.

Mind allows the scientific world to catalog in an orderly fashion what it has discovered.

Does mind then allow the scientific world to label its study as fact?

Mind, an intellectual faculty; mind as understanding, mind as memory, mind as opinion, mind as inclination, mind as purpose, mind the phenomenon beyond explaining.

Man has not been able to clearly define mind. He also cannot say with any certitude if the soul the spirit, the I, are all one and the same, just as he is unsure if mind and conscience are one. Does man realize he is asking mind to describe itself?

Man is carrying on his dialogue, but man has yet to reach the next level of mind. What he fails to take into the equation, what he overlooks, is that mind is leading the discourse, not man. Man is operating on the first level and mind is operating from a level man is not even aware of. It's like a dog chasing its tail. The dog will never catch the tail and man will never reach a final level for mind. Mind is infinite, man is finite, how can man even think he has hold of absolute knowledge, or absolute fact. There isn't any such thing.

Man, bases many of his decisions on the action of his brain, again he overlooks the physical element of this organ. It is finite. Man, by not choosing to see this, has already made his first mistake.

Man searches for a reality to hang his opinions on, but he uses as a base something that is not a reality. Man has begun on the wrong foot.

The sciences that seek to validate who they are, what they do, have overlooked the central focus, they are merely an activity of the mind they seek to interpret, to explain.

They seek true knowledge, but fail to see they seek it through mind. All they will receive is what mind deigns to give.

If the mind of man is the first level, and universal mind is the next level, what about mind as it applies to the other universes, the ones expanding, the new ones growing, the space without end? What about the ultimate level?

All the creations of man have originated in his mind, and yet man has never been able to out pace mind. Thought is mind in action.

Man is at square one, and it is exactly that, a square with parameters. Man must move out of the square, remove the parameters, and allow mind to move him forward.

Mind will always be ahead of man, because that which created mind, is beyond all that there is.

However, in moving mind out of the box and allowing it to roam free, man will be able to reach dimensions, levels, he only dreams about today.

521-MARC

# SEVENTY-THREE

## *ODDS AND ENDS OF THOUGHT*

The movement of life, elusive, tenacious, teacher and pupil.

No one can do for one what one must do for self. An axiom that seems to elude man. He continues to seek the answers to his questions, but tends to ignore them when they come. Man is looking for an easy way, and refuses to face the fact that there isn't one. Seeking the way is the way of self, seeking a way is the choice of ego.

No man can show his neighbor on how it is to be done, each must discover the way on his own. The universe has the wisdom, man must seek it within as well as without.

No man is another man's master, nor is he his guru.

Pearls of wisdom may be false pearls. It is up to each individual when he listens that he makes the distinction. Wisdomic guidelines are not the exclusive domain of any particular religious group. Each may have something to offer for the betterment of the human, the betterment of humankind, but the sieve of rational thought must be applied to all that one hears. The cruelest enemy of man is man himself. Listen, hear, learn, but keep in mind, altruism is a word and not everyone knows its definition.

There are world leaders who have their followers, and whose religion has endowed them with special powers, to name a few. The Pope, the Dalai Lama, the Ayatollah, any head of a specific group, etc. They impart their wisdomic words to their flock. One no different from the other except in the eyes of those who follow, who believe in the tenets, credo, dogma, of the espoused religion. Fighting words? No, words based on the fact that all were, are creations of man.

When such teachings emanate and are kept on the highest level possible and do not denigrate the followers than there may be value in what is taught.

Compassion must be shown as well as taught.

The brotherhood of man cannot advance itself if it is the brotherhood of Cain and Abel.

Power is an aphrodisiac and is at the root of man's inhumanity to man.

Violence and oppression are the result of power.

Communication, mutual understanding of man for man, must become an upswell beginning at the grassroots of man.

Money is not evil, it is what man chooses to do with it that causes problems.

Money is the province of all, but each must seek to acquire it for self, in a moral manner.

Each man on this planet is here for a purpose and the purpose is not clearly seen.

Each man is an individual, no matter what banner, ideology, etc., he finds himself pursuing. He will always be a singular entity.

The world, our planet, birthed diverse humankind. It will always remain one world, but it cannot ever be one nation, one country, or one ideology. The way of man, is not the way of the lemming.

The world will never be a world without problems. If man was given life, was given form and placed here to experience the lessons of life, he needs the problems to learn the lessons.

What man must learn, however, is the difference between his spiritual needs, and his materialistic wants. One attends to the development of the spirit, the other attends to the adornment of ego.

Man has the capability to stand back and observe himself in action, having this and seeing the action will be detrimental to him as well as others, why does he let the action continue?

Patience is a virtue, so is tolerance.

The star has many points, but it also has a center, so it should not be an impossibility for those with diverse views to attempt a convergence to the center.

Deep space is not only out where the galaxies are, it is also within each individual.

Teachers come and teachers go, one is indeed fortunate when one realizes he has found the perfect one.

There are not ten steps or fifty steps to enlightenment, to the Light. There is but one. When one takes that first step towards spiritual illumination, one does not need to count the ones to follow. One has already gained the insight. Mind has shown the way.

There are many schools of thought, but only end thought. To find the way, to follow the way, to become the way.

"To be or not to be?" was a question raised by Hamlet. It is also a question every spirit asks of itself when deciding whether to choose life as a human

Mind can generate all ones problems and mind can solve all ones problems.

Picture yourself as an empty vessel, then when you seek to fill that vessel fill it with only the good.

Be of concern about this lifetime, but do not forget about those to come. Live this one with such diligence that those that follow will believe they have found Paradise.

Today man seems to rely on anger, on rage, to get his way. This emotion generated by ego, has manifested many of the problems he faces in this life. The emotion of anger is a luxury, and man is finding out it is a luxury he cannot afford.

Gather not the treasures you perceive as important in this lifetime, they will not accompany you when the end point is reached. Nothing of the physical transcends.

We may all belong to the human race, but when we leave it we do so as a single entity.

We liberate the self within the human, so we can liberate the self of its cyclic inheritance.

Do not attempt to convert the world to your way of belief, your way is not the only way. Respect the way of the other.

In order to have world peace it must first begin within the self of each individual. If it is practiced internally it will spread like the ripples on water when a stone is cast.

It is time to turn the values, that are so predominant today, around. Responsibility, moral values, must be taught and the teaching must begin in the cradle. The self in the cradle has come here to learn.

# SEVENTY-FOUR

## *LIFE MOVES ON*

Life is a personal trip

~ ~ ~ ~ ~ ~

One makes the choices, one does the changing

~ ~ ~ ~ ~ ~

Do not allow things to just happen, take responsibility

~ ~ ~ ~ ~ ~

Failure is not failing unless one believes it is. It may only be that the timing is off or that one needs a new approach. To change is normal

~ ~ ~ ~ ~ ~

Buddhism teaches that we live in the moment. The journey we take, we take by inches, not miles, and it must be made with complete faith

~ ~ ~ ~ ~ ~

We control our lives, but He controls our "Life."

~ ~ ~ ~ ~ ~

One cannot make certain changes unless one makes them one's desire

~ ~ ~ ~ ~ ~

The winds of change blow in change

~ ~ ~ ~ ~ ~

"Life" goes on

~ ~ ~ ~ ~ ~

Self-pity is self-pity, it leads nowhere

~ ~ ~ ~ ~ ~

Friends will support one up to a point, but ultimately one
walks the rest of the way alone

~ ~ ~ ~ ~ ~

One must use one's talent, it is a precious gift

~ ~ ~ ~ ~ ~

One is a perfect spirit, it is the human being one is today
that is flawed

~ ~ ~ ~ ~ ~

Adversity is not a random event, or a change, of and by
itself. It is a choice made, a path followed, when the self
chose life

~ ~ ~ ~ ~ ~

We all have an inner voice, but some choose not to listen
to it

~ ~ ~ ~ ~ ~

Sit still and "Listen!"

~ ~ ~ ~ ~ ~

Giving up is the easy part, forging forward, regardless of
the circumstances takes guts

~ ~ ~ ~ ~ ~

Too many view life as a given, it is not, it is merely a glitch
in time

~ ~ ~ ~ ~ ~

"Dust to dust" is not an empty phrase, it tells the story of
the human life

~ ~ ~ ~ ~ ~

Do not put words into God's mouth.
Do not anticipate Him or His actions
Man is the mortal one

~ ~ ~ ~ ~ ~

We grow with choice
Life is our job, we must work with it, not at it

~ ~ ~ ~ ~ ~

The angel looking over ones shoulder, is the angel one is

~ ~ ~ ~ ~ ~

We say we have "needs," but an evaluation of those needs
soon shows us they are merely "wants"

~ ~ ~ ~ ~ ~

We are told to open our heart to God, God already owns
it and lives within it. What we need to open is the door
to the pride of self and eliminate pride

~ ~ ~ ~ ~ ~

Why is the question, "Isn't there more to life?" being
asked? Isn't the fact that one has life enough? It is what
one chooses to do with it that defines it.

~ ~ ~ ~ ~ ~

Life is a preparation for fulfillment. Fulfillment comes
when one crosses the threshold into the Light

~ ~ ~ ~ ~ ~

We are not Gods, but we are the pinpoints of God's Light

~ ~ ~ ~ ~ ~

To attach oneself to material things is to ignore the fact
that such things will inevitably be let behind. Anything of
a physical nature cannot make it over the threshold. Only
spirit can make the trip

~ ~ ~ ~ ~ ~

God does not take sides

~ ~ ~ ~ ~ ~

What happens on the outside has already been planned
on the inside

~ ~ ~ ~ ~ ~

Lemmings travel unerringly to the sea, mortal man,
whether he realizes it or not, accepts it or not, travels
unerringly toward that well-known threshold
Must one kneel, always, in prayer? Hardly.
God does not demand it.
Prayer does not originate in the knees, it originates in the

self and all mortals may not be capable of kneeling. Those
ill in bed, those in a wheelchair, whatever. Does God not
accept their prayers?
Prayer is from the inner self and it is through the self that
it makes its way to God

~ ~ ~ ~ ~ ~

Does God reveal himself the minute one crosses over the
threshold, inadvertently or as a final step?
Or is He a holographic vision?
Crossing is only one step up the ladder that one must
take before one comes into the Presence.
There is a ladder, there is a spiral, one must keep journey-
ing upward.
One may see a light when one crosses, but it is not "The
Light."
To see the Ultimate Light demands one have reached
perfection

~ ~ ~ ~ ~ ~

We all have a fear. We all fear . . . something
The fear is a self-made fear, it is a choice man makes.
We take an action and we decide to choose . . . fear

~ ~ ~ ~ ~ ~

Too many people want life to be a breeze and yet even a
breeze can turn into a bad wind

~ ~ ~ ~ ~ ~

It is easy to set goals, it is not so easy to keep them
Patience may be a virtue, but one must look at the context
in which patience is placed

~ ~ ~ ~ ~ ~

Fear and worry go hand in hand

~ ~ ~ ~ ~ ~

The today, that became yesterday, came and went, the
anticipated tomorrow will never arrive.
Yesterday, tomorrow, are always today

~ ~ ~ ~ ~ ~

We must count life in seconds, because it is in the second
that it is

~ ~ ~ ~ ~ ~

No one else can provide the guidance one needs
Their path is not the path that one must take

~ ~ ~ ~ ~ ~

There are many kinds of courage, but the one with the
most import is the courage to live life

~ ~ ~ ~ ~ ~

God plays a major part in each and every life,
He allows one free will,
He allows one choice on how one wishes to conduct oneself

~ ~ ~ ~ ~ ~

Faith is the driver, without faith one is rudderless

~ ~ ~ ~ ~ ~

We should live life as it unfolds before us, we should not
wait until the end of it to realize and appreciate just how
wonderful it was

~ ~ ~ ~ ~ ~

Let go and let God
There is a prayer named the "Desiderata"
It is also called the "Serenity Prayer" and it reads like this:

God grant me the serenity to accept the things I cannot
change;
Courage to change the things I can;
And the wisdom to know the difference.
Living one day at a time;
Enjoying one moment at a time;
Accepting hardships as the
Pathway to Peace;
Taking as He did this sinful world as it is;
Not as I would have it;
Trusting that He will make all things right if I surrender to
His will;

That I may be reasonably happy in this life and supremely
happy with Him forever in the next.
Amen

~ ~ ~ ~ ~ ~

A prayer many of us wish we had written, but Reinhold
Niebuhr is its author.
A lovely poem, heartfelt, it begins with a plea to God for
the benefit of a mere mortal, and his ego.
All one need ask of God is a continuing faith in a life eternal.
Without faith all the rest is meaningless

~ ~ ~ ~ ~ ~

A prayer is a prayer
A psalm is a psalm
A hymn is a hymn
What do they have in common?
They were, and are, composed and written, by the human.
It is not their prayer, their psalm, their hymn, that will
open the door.
It is one's own heartfelt composition, recited by one, that
has the most meaning.
Parroting words written by others is using someone else's
coattails in order to arrive someplace

~ ~ ~ ~ ~ ~

One may feel one does not know the way, but God does,
He is waiting to guide

~ ~ ~ ~ ~ ~

It is not the main highway, but all the little byways, that
provide one with the experiences of life

~ ~ ~ ~ ~ ~

To choose is up to one
To make a decision is up to one
To take action is up to one
To get results is up to one

~ ~ ~ ~ ~ ~

It is up to us to remember that the walk we take, and not

the walk someone else takes, that will get us where we
wish to go

~ ~ ~ ~ ~ ~

From little acorns great oaks grow or as Emile Coué put it,
"Every day, in every way,
I'm getting better and better"

~ ~ ~ ~ ~ ~

The acorn has but one job, to grow into the best oak tree
it can.
We all have but one job, to live the gift called life to the
best of our ability

~ ~ ~ ~ ~ ~

Life is the drum, we are the drummers, and each of us
must march to our own beat

~ ~ ~ ~ ~ ~

We must not live our life according to the buzzwords of
society.
Self-esteem, texture, color, victim, this, that, are not what
give life meaning.
We, as individuals, can only do that.
Society cannot provide for one, one can only provide for
self.

~ ~ ~ ~ ~ ~

The play is ours . . .
The role is ours . . .
The action is ours . . .
The applause belongs to us

~ ~ ~ ~ ~ ~

Yes, "Life" is what one makes it

~ ~ ~ ~ ~ ~

The movement of life . . . A force
The force . . . The river of life
The river . . . The energy of life

~ ~ ~ ~ ~ ~

Life is us, we are life

Printed in the United States
3370